PASSING A
GOOD TIME

PASSING A GOOD TIME

*With Guns, Dogs, Fly Rods,
and Other Joys*

by
Gene Hill

Illustrations by
Tom Hennessey

Countrysport Press
Traverse City, Michigan

All of the chapters of this book first appeared in somewhat
different form in *Field & Stream* magazine.

This edition of *Passing a Good Time* was designed by Angela Saxon
of Saxon Design, Traverse City, Michigan.
The text is set in Berling.

Third Edition
10 9 8 7 6 5 4 3

Published by Countrysport Press LLC
Building 116, Craig Industrial Park, Selma, Alabama 36701

Printed in the United States of America

Library of Congress Cataloging-in-Publication Data

Hill, Gene.
    Passing a good time : with guns, dogs, fly rods, and other joys /
by Gene Hill ; illustrations by Tom Hennessey. — 1st ed.
    p.   cm.
    ISBN 0-924357-64-9 (trade). — ISBN 0-924357-65-7 (limited
ed. of 250)
    1. Hunting—Anecdotes. 2. Fishing—Anecdotes.   I. Title.
SK33.H6596   1996
799.2973—dc21   96-48148
                                                 CIP

This is for Cathy Lee—

WELDING, LIVE BAIT, NOTARY,
WILLS, AND GEN'L REPAIRS

Everything I always wanted…

CONTENTS

FOREWORD

It is 1946, months after the cessation of the global agonies of World War II. On the sweltering Pacific island of Okinawa, a young sandy-haired American squints into the sun as he stands guard over a small group of Japanese POWs as they go through the desultory chores that occupy their days while waiting to be returned to their homeland. The soldier has nothing particular on his mind, except returning to his native hills of northern New Jersey and beginning his postponed college education. He does not realize that he has become complacent—and vulnerable.

Suddenly, one of the prisoners lunges into the eighteen-year-old, knocking him down, ripping his .45 automatic from the holster. Shocked, numb with disbelief, the American stares into the barrel of the .45 as the Japanese jerks at the trigger repeatedly. The gun does not fire. The action has not been pulled back to put a round into the chamber.

As the prisoner fumbles with the pistol in frustration, the American smashes into him and regains his weapon. He slides back the action, chambering a bullet, and aims into the face of the now-cringing POW.

The soldier's mind screams with fury over his humiliating failure and near-defeat. His finger touches the trigger.

Then the moment passes. Trembling hands lower the pistol. There will be no blood on these sands this day.

The lucky American soldier made it back to New Jersey, and from there to Harvard and on to a career in advertising, chiefly on the Ford account. He also became a writer whose works are treasured as few others, particularly among the brethren for whom the call of the great outdoors runs as deep as blood itself.

Gene Hill will probably be somewhat embarrassed by my retelling of his "war story." He seldom mentions the incident, even to his closest friends. I'm sure he feels that other things are a lot more important. But for myself, I cannot help reflecting on what we all would have been denied had the name Gene Hill been added to the casualty lists, or had the sudden act of revenge scarred his mind.

To me, coming to a new Gene Hill book is like heading up the familiar steps of a favorite hunting or fishing camp, where one of my best friends is waiting inside. Every time I have the pleasure of his company, Gene Hill has stuff to say that I want to hear. And the book you have in front of you right now is no exception.

What I treasure most about Gene's work is the subtle way his prose can jump-start my own memories and re-ignite all the emotions I went afield to find in the first place. The pleasures of hunting and fishing, or even a quiet walk through good country, leap from the pages of Gene Hill's books like grouse whirring from cover or tarpon tailwalking across the flats. Sometimes the images seem to quietly drift into one's consciousness the same way that clouds struck by the light of the setting sun make you pause…and notice.

From the first day he picked up a gun or fishing rod, Gene Hill has never forgotten that the joys of hunting and fishing are best pursued with a light heart and as much humility as pride. That the skills which we seek to master can never really be mastered at all. Whatever tastes of perfection we enjoy from time to time are earned through the integrity of sportsmanship and understanding. They cannot be purchased at any price.

To show you what I'm talking about, I offer the following tidbits from the pages ahead—hors d'oeuvres, if you will, from *Passing a Good Time*.

SNORING

"Anyone can snore at times—even I have been accused, mistakenly, of course. Unfortunately, there are no hard and fast rules, and a man who isn't really a snorer can suddenly come into his own and keep as many as three rooms awake in a hunting or fishing camp. Russian roulette is what we're talking about—sooner or later, at one camp or another, you have to lose."

ON BEING AN EXPERT

"Why bother learning the Bimini Twist when experts are shoving each other out of the way to tie one for you to prove that they know how and you don't? Why bother to sharpen your knife when in your four-man tent three fellow Nimrods have brought eleven kinds of stones and exotic oils? By the second day they've sharpened all their stuff, including the kindling ax, and will grab hold of your knives like a preacher embracing a sinner."

SOME OF "GENE'S GEMS"

"Whenever you find something you really like, buy two, or three, before they change it or stop making it."

"The more remote a gas station is, the earlier it closes. It will never be open on Sundays."

"Why do so many of us think that good equipment is a substitute for practice?"

"The best shooting instructor is a case of shells."

The big dramatic moments of hunting and fishing—those in which we perhaps come close to bagging "the most" or "the biggest"—are few compared to the myriad small pleasures that we can experience with a rod or gun in our hands. And often, as Gene suggests, these special memories become "hidden away" beneath the pressures and time schedules of daily living. But we know they are there, to be savored and shared on occasion, especially when a new Gene Hill book comes along and reminds us not only of how fortunate indeed we have been in the past, but what we can look forward to our next time out.

Lamar Underwood

Editor's Note: Lamar Underwood is former editor-in-chief of Sports Afield *and* Outdoor Life. *Currently, he is editorial director of the* Outdoor Magazine Group *of Harris Publications, Inc., in New York City.*

1

THE OUTDOOR WRITERS

I've never liked the phrase "outdoor writer." It has the connotation of a poet writing odes to the wind or verses in praise of nature, not someone who addresses important outdoor subjects, like guns and dogs and trout and bass and the people who delight in pursuing fish and game.

My attraction to this field was the result of early exposure to some very good and very knowledgeable writers. I was quickly impressed with the clean and direct style of Jack O'Connor, and later on when I got to know Jack personally, we spent a lot of time on the subject of what good writing was. Jack had been a professor of English and held some strong opinions that I agree with. As the dean of gun writers then, Jack made a point of never writing down to his audience and he had that special ability to leave his reader with the feeling that he had been along with Jack on some adventure and had enjoyed himself immensely. John Jobson, who wrote mostly about camping, had the same wonderful story-telling touch and although he was strongly opinionated, like O'Connor, you knew it was from personal experience—they had been there and had taken you along with them. Such writers are rare indeed and I continue to envy the deft touch they had with the written word.

I was, and am, taken by the blend of humor, truth, and teaching in the writings of Corey Ford, Robert Ruark, and Gordon McQuarrie. Those men were masters at introducing us to their friends, their home country, and a strong sense of ethics. They showed us, by personal examples, how to respect our sport and to bring to it a feeling of wonder and care. They exhorted us to be serious but not overly so, to regard our *time* with guns and dogs and rods and the people that come with them as a period of grace that enriches us in a very special way.

I always found an undercurrent of almost spiritual guiding in the work of these writers—an endless series of examples of the justness and generosity learned in the field, and why it should be extended to our everyday lives. Real sportsmen aren't born that way; they must be nurtured and taught. These writers, each in his own way, taught millions of us what was right and what was not. It's interesting to note that most of these writers had varied careers. Some were highly regarded novelists, others were well-known journalists, screenwriters, teachers, and essayists. And in their work for the sporting magazines they, like all good professionals, gave us the best they had.

The pioneering of new frontiers has always played an important role in the literature of the outdoors. Lee Wulff was one of the pioneers and he brought the art of fishing for trout and salmon to a new level. He changed not only the way we fished, but how we looked at fishing and at the fish themselves. He gave "sport fishing" a whole new definition and he put a "priceless" tag on the worth of our fish. Along with the new concept of light tackle and the self-limitations he preached and practiced, Lee wrote about the pioneering of new places and the magic of the small plane.

While Lee took us to Canada's Atlantic provinces, Joe Brooks brought the wonders of Argentina to us, and A. J. McClane, returned from the death and destruction of World War II, introduced us to new ways to fish with light tackle for tarpon, permit, and bonefish.

The new ethics of fishing were borne on the work of these writers. We learned that "how many" was no longer the fisherman's credo, or shouldn't be. These writers changed the way and the why we fished almost overnight. That is what good writing is supposed to do—stretch the horizons of the mind. I still can't read anything that McClane wrote without feeling both envious and humble. He wrote with an intelligent enthusiasm and with such sparkling language and respect for his subject that his work is unique in the truest sense of the word.

I know it's obvious, but a writer has to write about *something*. And good writers like a challenge equal to their skills. Fishing and shooting are harder to write about than you might think. The writers I admire have taken me with them, in print, and showed me how things work. They made me dream, gave me something to look forward to, and left me with a lot to reflect on.

You think I've forgotten Ed Zern? Not a chance. To my way of thinking, no one has been as original, or as genuinely funny, wise, or incisive. Ed taught me to find my own voice. He brought to us all a much needed and welcome way of saying that as long as we're here, let's have a good time. In other words, no one who is vain or pompous or greedy or mean should be allowed in our clubhouse.

Ed Zern once turned to me when we were fishing and I was in one of my sloppy casting modes, and said: "Hill, what the hell are you thinking about?"

Well, Ed, I'm thinking about how to thank you and all the others who took the time to write for us— telling us how it ought to be done, and knowing that we wouldn't do it as well, but encouraging us just the same.

2

THE GOOD OLD DAYS

Back when a hunting license cost $1 and you wore it pinned to your hat, few of us fooled with grouse and woodcock with any serious intent. We were simply *hunting-starved* after the spring and summer.

There was an unofficial birdhunter badge awarded by the "retired" who hung around the hardware store. "Them boys can't wait to get out," one old fellow would say. "Walk all the way up and back to Burnt Swamp just for partridges. Got one or two last week, I hear."

"Damn fools is what I say," another would comment. But this was back when being a damn fool wasn't a bad thing. The trick was to grow out of it and "amount to something."

None of us had bird dogs. Whatever "trained" dogs we saw arrived in fancy cars, squired by men wearing knee-high leather boots with their britches tucked in, asking the sort of questions about birds that made it seem as if we didn't share a common language.

Our grouse hunting technique was simple. One of us would walk an old woods road and the other would meander on a parallel path through whatever looked like good bird cover. Abandoned apple orchards were our favorite, probably as much for the fruit as the birds. There were a lot more abandoned apple trees than you'd think; either I grew up in a very unlucky part of the world, or the early settlers weren't as provident as they might have been.

The grouse gun of choice was the "household shotgun." This was one-gun country. If it was a single-barrel pump, it was the Model 97 Winchester, a side-by-side was likely to be a Baker or a Smith, with the odd LeFever showing up occasionally.

Guns in the $50 class were the high norm; there were a lot of cheap single-shot hammer guns with names like Batavia, Crescent, or Woodlander. More often than not the receiver was wrapped with wire or bicycle tape.

If a shooter is given a second or so of warning, a partridge gliding over an open track isn't the most difficult wing shot, and though unskilled, we managed to provide a decent dinner every now and then. Our mothers would talk as if it were everyday stuff, which embarrassed us in front of the men. Still, the seeds of reputation were planted that way and the legend of the local grouse hunter grew, no matter how slender the basis in fact.

Woodcock were just hunted. We couldn't "drive" them, so we just plain got into the coverts and shot at what we flushed. We didn't do much harm to the species. It was a matter of who was lucky and who wasn't.

No one I knew particularly liked to hunt or eat wood-cock except for me.

The king of game birds was the ringneck pheas-ant, a rooster, of course, brought proudly home smoothed and unruffled. If there was a place to hang roosters where they could be seen from the road, that's where they were hung. Our birds were not really native, although a few managed to survive the harsh winter. So the ethic of classic wingshooting had only a slippery handhold, and a pheasant, unless grandly described as "shot flying," was assumed to have been gathered in a less dignified way. Even then, after the first few days, roosters were very hard to come by. They were birds of opportunity and as such were treated as joyously as found money. When they were plucked, every feather was saved; the ladies made hatbands, and artistic arrangements of tail feathers were placed in care-fully sited vases.

But the real hunting season, the one we looked forward to most for food and sport, wasn't birds at all; it was rabbits. They were abundant and reliable. You could go it alone, or with your dog, or with a pal or a gang. You could claim arcane hunting skills by taking most of your rabbits sitting, for example...the quarry was unaware due to your uncanny stealth and wood-craft. To be honest, few hunts are more fun than mix-ing up beagles with brushpiles and few meals more tasty than fried rabbit with biscuits or cornbread.

A rabbit dog was any dog that would roust out a bunny. A *real* rabbit dog, which not many of us had, was a beagle. I once had a bassett that followed me home (really). He wasn't much good on rabbits, but we took him out once in a while because he really enjoyed it. I don't remember ever not having a dog close by, including at school where they slept on the porch waiting for us.

I'm delighted that technology has not tainted the world of the rabbit hunter. No decoys, no plastic carrots, no lettuce scent, no briar patch camo. I suspect real rabbit hunters would reject it anyway. The real rabbit hunter is at his prime when he's about eleven or twelve years old, and I'll bet that when he brings home a rabbit for supper, cleaned and quartered just right, the lady of the house still lets him know he's something special. And I wouldn't be surprised if his "rabbit dog" slept just at the edge of the bed—and that his dreams of a white Christmas always included a nice tracking snow.

3

HUNTER'S
BLOOD

Not long ago, a reviewer of a book on fly fishing made a comment or two on catch-and-release and then went on to remark that millions were to be made by the person who came up with a laser beam or the like to give hunters the same privilege.

I don't think so.

There are more differences between fishing and hunting—catching fish and killing game—than there are similarities. First, and perhaps most important, a human hunter is *himself* an animal. He shares a lot of the mammalian genetics of his prey. And he can *identify* with an elk or a grizzly or a deer, something he can't really do with a fish, however majestic.

Fishing is fun. Lose a fish and you can always find something to laugh at, to make light about. But hunting is always serious. Wound an animal, no matter how small, and a darkness clouds the mind. There is a charming, artistic mystery about a Royal Wulff; hefting a 180-grain .30/06 cartridge, or a 12-gauge load of 8s, sends a very different message.

No doubt I have written often, and truthfully, that as I've held a quail or grouse, I've wished I could breathe the life back into it and let it fly away. But it takes the finality of death to make hunting fulfilling, something beyond good or bad, right or wrong, sorrow or repenting. This is the ultimate paradox.

In recent years both hunters and fishermen have taken on more difficult challenges in order to maintain the idea of sport. Primitive weapons like longbows and blackpowder guns are coming back, and there is a resurgence in small-bore shotguns, lighter, finer lines, barbless hooks, and the like. All this to foster the feeling of parity, of wit and skill, instead of force and power. So we say. But for hunters, the end is the same for those who kill. The deer is still dead and whether or not the hunter can handle this in his heart is very much an individual thing. I see flaws in the arguments put forth by hunters and fishermen who insist that the greater the challenge, the more sporting it is. I understand, mind you, but I don't always agree with the rationale.

With the carrying of a gun, a person commits himself or herself to knowing what happens when it goes off. Whether you are smoking a trap target or tumbling a high crossing mallard, they have in common a very visible and satisfying result. It comes right down to instincts and obscure ganglia we often don't know we have until the shot is taken. I remember shooting sand grouse in Africa a while back. My tracker, who was disturbingly blasé when I took an antelope at 200 yards, was almost uncontrollable with wonder at my

magical ability to bring down a pair of high birds. One shot had the element of great mystery, perhaps, and one didn't.

I feel very much the same way. And I confess that I would not be satisfied with hitting the birds—clay or feathered—with the beam of some harmless, high-tech laser or flashlight compared to an ounce of 7s. It would be like playing pinball with no bells or flashing scoreboard.

A fair number of fishermen consider their skills exercised once they have coaxed a fish into taking a lure. I disagree. I need to feel the contact with the fish that follows the hookup. I need a conclusion, a story that says *The End* when it's over. Then I can release the fish with deep satisfaction, playing some petty god. As for hunting, I need to go beyond calling the big tom close enough to see him blink, or stalking a deer until it's almost close enough to touch, or bringing a bunch of Canadas into the blocks. "Almost" isn't good enough; I need to take the final step.

There is, of course, the simple bio math. So many acres, so many deer. It makes sense to "harvest" game as they now like to say. I dislike the falsity of the word "harvest" in this context, no matter how carefully it is used. I don't think you can harvest something you didn't put there for that purpose. It's all right to argue with me—everyone else does—but this is merely putting another face on the same thing, an apology where none is needed.

For myself, if I didn't hunt with some degree of deadly earnestness, I would not hunt at all. When I broke my first fifty straight at skeet, someone grabbed my hat and the squad all had a shot at it. When at age eleven I killed my first buck, an old hunting partner, part Blackfoot, reached into the deer, wiped his hands on my face, and told me that I was a hunter. I've forgotten what happened to the riddled hat, but I still remember my first taste of hunter's blood.

4

THE

SEASON

For the hunter, the months of fall tend to merge into a special period of time and a state of mind called "the season." It might be bird season or big game; and for a lot of us, it's both. Certainly it's time to see how the new pup is coming along or if old Jack can still do the hills with us. The road may be a little longer than we remembered, the cover a little harder to walk through, or it may all be downhill with the wind behind you. But no matter how much it's all brand new or how much it's reliving a memory, the season is the right time of the year to be in the right places.

For the few of us who can just once resist the incredibly strong urge to second guess our guide or mentor, the big buck will indeed appear where we were told and he'll become ingrained in our bittersweet memories. Even fewer of us will make a shot at a grouse roaring through the clearing on *our* side of the cover where the sight of a wisp of drifting feathers will be ours alone.

The kid with the single-shot will see the pheasant he's dreamed about, flushing from his feet in a towering climb. His mother will see a different boy than she fussed over that morning and his father will put the tail feathers in a special place without saying too much about it.

No doubt I'll be in the wrong place at the right time, a spot I'm all too familiar with. Since I'm less than a sure thing on right-to-left crossing shots, you know which side of the tree most of my birds choose. I've learned to smile—but don't read my lips.

But a lot of wrong places turn out to be right. A day washed away lets you listen to the tapping of the rain on a cabin window that frames a thousand private scenes. When it's getting a little bit darker than you'd like in new country and the North Star isn't exactly where it ought to be, finding a deer trail that leads back to the truck gives you a special sense of place.

Sometimes the right place is as new and fresh as a page in an unread book; and sometimes it is safe and sure, like a favorite poem. I've done a lot of hunting as an excuse to explore, and why not. Not all the things we want are external, not all the reasons we go out are measured by number or size. We hunt to see things in a different way; the hunter at sunset is not the same as he was at dawn.

The places of the season are different than they are the rest of the year. The sleepy swamp pond is quick with a clattering of mallards. The rank alder bottom is host to a flight of woodcock probing for worms. The later afternoon light in the old orchard glows on a handful of deer searching the dry grass for the last of the fallen apples. In the high meadow, the bull elk listens to a distant bugle and watches the cows for signs of nervousness.

The *bob-white, bob-white* at evening is a little more urgent during the season. In the short days of fall the pace quickens; nights are colder and the tension mounts. The owls and the foxes make their rounds and the dark parts in their path. The hunter feels it too, watching the English setter tense and rumble in her dreams. The last of the fire reminds him of roosters floating up from orange-tinted briars. He remembers his first deer, wonders about his last, makes a selfish wish, and goes to bed smiling at the thought of tomorrow, when he can walk away from what some people call the real world and step once again into *the season*.

5

RIVER
REFLECTIONS

A good fisherman learns to "think" like a fish. He can really *see* the rainbow trout living under that cut bank where the cottonwood leans out, holding on to the rock ledge with long root fingers. He can *feel* the trout seeking the comfort of a roof overhead, always vigilant for trespass from above.

Nor do surface signs escape the eyes and mind of a good fisherman. He knows the way the current eddies, how nymphs move through the water, the skirmishes of foraging baitfish, the silhouettes of ants and hoppers, caddisflies, and mayflies drifting in the river's flow.

A *very* good fisherman can sense the fear and the boldness and the urgency that a trout must live with to survive—the heron stalking in the shallows, the osprey gliding overhead, the mink and the otter hunting in the shadows. Like the trout, a very good fisherman knows that in a river, everything must be weighed and measured because instinct and life are the same, and one mistake is the ultimate error.

The concept of a river is difficult for me to grasp fully. I know a little about it, I guess at a little of it, and I add a touch of wishful thinking and hope. My streamer fly book is a colorful reflection of all these thoughts. For no special reason except habit and optimism, I usually start with a Grey Ghost. I think "swimming minnow" and make my cast slightly upstream and across, letting the current play the fly as if it were alive. Intent as a starvling, I stare at the darting lure, watching out of the corner of my eye the place where the trout must surely lie. And then he's there, white belly flashing as he rolls and tosses his head in anger and fear. I play the fish, then hold him in my hand, not really understanding what it is I've done. It seems right to whisper something very private as I watch him swim away.

A better fisherman would have expected all this to happen; in fact, he might have thought my trout too easy and looked for a greater challenge. But I, like the trout, have to do what I can where and when I can do it. Nothing in trout fishing is really easy for me, except looking backward, in retrospect.

It's easy to remember all the times I was wrong; a poor choice of fly, the bad casts, striking too early, *ad infinitum* and *nauseum*. I wonder about time on the river, and about how many casts I have left before the last one. Then an osprey misses its dive and I know I'm not alone.

When a good fisherman can't move a trout into taking a fly, he will try something different—another fly, another angle of presentation, challenging the trout to resist his skills. I look for another trout, one less learned, one I can meet on a more equal footing.

Given the choice, I prefer fishing wet flies. There's a kind of mystery about fishing "blind" under the surface that intrigues me, maybe because it suits my ability and imagination. It seems I can "see" my fly working in my mind's eye. I am not the type to spend much time working out delicate casts and adjusting to eliminate even the least bit of drag. I belong to the "big fly, big fish" school, although I probably haven't progressed much beyond the third grade. But I am not on the river to catch fish as much as I am out to be fishing. A lot of other things are going on along the river that pleasure me as much as a trout taking a fly, which is certainly the stubborn rationale of a third-grader.

I do, however, envy the good fisherman. He fishes what he believes will take fish; if he has prejudices, he's learned to control them. I wish I had faith and confidence in more than a Grey Ghost or a Royal Wulff. I wish I had the insight to know where a trout was most likely to be and why and what will fetch him out. I don't even like to think very long about the good fisherman's mastery of technique—the long cast placed just so, the dragless, imperceptible float of his dry fly, the metronomic sweepings of his casts transecting a pool. And all of this accompanied by the constant splash of hooked fish. For this skilled angler the only real silence is when he is resting or changing flies.

I watch the good fisherman. I read his books. I buy the same rods and reels and weigh down the identical vest with the identical paraphernalia. But there are so many other differences, like talent and insight for openers. The good fisherman is surprised when he doesn't catch fish; I am just the other way around. Still, it's comforting to know that both of us see a trout river as a magic kingdom, and we are both always thinking about the next cast and the next turn in the river.

6

DABBLING IN EXPERTISE

I was reading the obituary of a man I once knew slightly and was surprised to see him referred to as someone who'd been "considered a complete sportsman."

As far as I knew, this fellow had fished a bit, done a little bird hunting, and in college dabbled with the sailing team. Like millions of other men he enjoyed the odd sporting pursuit, but I hadn't ever thought of him as "complete." Then I began wondering *who* among my acquaintances really is or was a complete sportsman. And, more to the point, how does one define *complete sportsman?*

Look at it this way: how many hats do most of us outdoorsmen wear? Just being a skilled hunter or fisherman, or both, really isn't enough. One also needs special qualities, like high levels of woodcraft, and boating knowledge, and certainly the ability to survive in odd places at bad times. The basics of botany, ornithology, and biology would also impress me, not to mention the need for proficiency in skinning, horse-manship, and having "a map in your head." I'd also like to be able to tie a few good fly patterns, really know how to read strange water, be a lot more comfortable with a compass, and feel more prepared to deal with the unexpected when it comes to weather. So far, those skills seem to have eluded me.

I think the complete sportsman ought to have trained a decent dog or two, know how to treat a sick rifle or shotgun, put a keen edge on an axe or knife, and mend the ordinary stuff that tends to break. No names, of course, but the complete sportsman never forgets his rain jacket or pocket knife, and never leaves his license at home on the dresser. His knots don't come undone and he never runs out of gas or money. (I'll forgive him any two of the above if he doesn't snore!)

When you stop to think about it, the very idea of lumping hunters and fishermen together under the *sportsman* banner is a relatively recent development. I'd say the idea really gained momentum in the 1930s with the imposition of strict bag limits and a lessening need to hunt for food. Pleasure and satisfaction became the main reasons to be afield, and the way we hunted and fished became more important than the result. The pictures of men with neckties and a brace of dogs, sporting double-barreled Foxes and Parkers and L. C. Smiths replaced those of camp game poles hung with carcasses of deer, or Model T Fords peeking out from under dozens of canvasbacks and mallards, or stringers of trout. We were playing by new rules, some of which were instituted in honor of the quarry.

My own introduction to "fair chase" was a hickory switch wielded by my father when he saw me shoot a swimming duck. It was a brief introduction, right to the point, and the accompanying lecture on ethics was equally direct. (His "hunter's safety course" was conducted the same way and completed to our mutual satisfaction in about two minutes.)

Given today's strictures on time, money, and opportunity, we tend to let *complete* cover the sportsman who loads his own bullets for the '06, spends a little time on the skeet field, takes a week or two someplace gunning birds with his own dog, and gets in some time on his favorite fishing water. I know a few sportsmen, but not many, who really do know how to build a small cooking fire, pitch a lean-to, saddle a horse, track a specific elk or deer, build a blind, or confidently get from point A to point B and back again. To be discouragingly honest, there are far too many modern hunters and fishermen who can't walk through the woods without sounding like a platoon, who talk too much in the field or on the water, carry too much useless stuff, and ignore which way the wind is blowing. These folks too are complete, but I can't complete the sentence among gentlemen.

Obviously I like the idea of being a complete sportsman. I'd also like to be able to play the guitar and run fifty straight more often than Halley's comet appears. So, like most of us, I stick with the stuff I'm good at—or at least not awful. I have a good double gun and now and then do it some justice. I have had ducks come in to my decoys and have trained a dog to go get the few that didn't flare. I can throw a fly and a spoon or plug, rig up some live baits, and run white water in a canoe—if it isn't too white! Once upon a time I made spending money with a trap line, and although I've always been a little confused, I've never been really lost, at least not yet. I know this is a little on the slim side considering the amount of time I've spent dodging honest work, but I've enjoyed every minute of it—even when I've forgotten my rain gear or lost my car keys. I mean, nobody's perfect.

7

FLY BUM

For those of you who are historically minded and might like to see the one and only trout fly I have ever tied, it's on display at North Fork Outfitters in Island Park, Idaho. I tied it for Roger Keckeissen (under the guidance of his wife) to prove that I am not *all* thumbs. If you know what a Pale Morning Dun looks like and if you are imaginative, you will probably recognize it.

Since this experiment in fly tying took the better part of an hour, you'll understand why I rely on the kindness of others to keep my fly box fairly well stocked. I have heard hundreds of fishermen preach that tying flies is half the fun, and I don't doubt it is the best way to learn to identify both fly patterns and insects. My ignorance in these matters is lamentable but unavoidable—sort of like my manual dexterity, which is only in demand for loosening nuts or opening bottles.

I do tie most of the common fishing knots—I have a masterful touch on nail knots—since I'm embarrassed to ask anyone else to tie them for me. I will also admit that it takes me somewhat longer than most people to bend an improved clinch, but I haven't lost more than six or eight fish because the knot came undone, and I lost those fish a long time ago.

When I was trapping, I constantly wore a tell-tale black-and-blue ring around my right thumb where I was slow or clumsy in getting out of the way of my Oneidas and Blake & Lambs. My father, who had a warped sense of humor and who could set traps in the dark, was not above calling me "Lefty," since I often went to some trouble to avoid using my sore right hand. I was forever banished to right field in baseball and came to know that "The Iron Glove" is not always a flattering remark.

Consequently, my life has been forced into narrow channels and my dreams of becoming a surgeon, concert pianist, or professional crocheter never materialized. Instead, I've had to develop a large compensatory sense of cunning; although overly engineered by nature for brute work, for some reason I have an aversion to it.

I learned early on that a person who ties flies, secretly or not so secretly, believes that his work is at least outstanding. No matter if his creations shed down to the bare hook in six casts, he views each one as if it were a special child. It's important to know that such people are, secretly or not so secretly, anxious for praise and flattery. If you tell a fly tier that never have you seen such a perfectly proportioned, delicate, ephemeral work of art as his size 16 Adams, he will force a dozen or so on you and would be dashed, if not miserable, should you refuse.

Rather than hurt a tier's feelings, I always accept, but never without remarking that if the Adams is so incomparable, I dare not even *imagine* what perfection he might achieve were he to whip up a batch of Joe's Hoppers or Irresistibles—which happen to be two patterns that I never have enough of.

On rare occasions, I have actually had to pay money for flies, usually the less common Atlantic salmon patterns, but I find it difficult to use them and end up tossing them into a drawer; I have almost a dozen. By buying flies, I know that I've somehow denied someone, somewhere, the warm sense of satisfaction that can only come through the act of giving. Actually, it's selfish of me to buy flies, so when I feel a moment of weakness coming on, I force myself to satisfy my urge to spend by picking up a small dispenser of tippet material or a tube of glue.

This generosity on my part, however, does exact its price. I remain shamefully ignorant of all but a few of the commonest fly patterns. More than once someone has opened his fly box at streamside and said, "There's a hatch of damselflies due shortly; take a few and be ready." Not knowing a damselfly from a caddis case, I hesitate as charmingly and as unsuspiciously as I can, and say, "I'd feel better about this if you picked them out—they're all so perfect." Not only do I get the right fly, but where I would only have taken half a dozen, he, stout fellow that he is, will in all likelihood hand over eight or ten.

Of course in a few days I will have forgotten what a damselfly looks like and will have to offer my box and suggest to someone that they take *one* (I stress *one*) so that I can then tie the same thing on with an air of knowing all along. I most commonly get caught up in this situation when I ask for a #6 Blue Charm and my companion says he gave me a handful last time we fished together. Sometimes I can get around things by saying I thought his flies were too good to use and I'm thinking of having them framed as part of my estate. But that will only work once or twice on the same fly tier during a single season; nothing is foolproof.

The fly tier is, to those of us who don't tie, what a doctor is to those who don't practice medicine—a person of needed skills, a dedicated, selfless angel of mercy. I grow misty-eyed when I remember the devotion of the tier who stays up long past his bedtime, bent over the vise, his learned fingers patiently doing what has to be done so that I can face the morning rise without fear.

What little I can do to repay them I do gladly. Fulsome praise, a certain amount of toadying, and ready access to any spirits I might have in camp. If you share my need and are drawn, like me, to the camp tier as a moth to a flame, don't forget that no matter how shabby the fly, the man just might know what he's doing. So when he shyly offers you the fruits of his labor, remember my motto:

"Just say *yes*."

8

WONDERFUL
WORLD

If all of us could really shoot the shotguns we love the most—it would be a wonderful world. But shotguns can be willful, capricious, whimsical, obdurate, and unpredictable. Like most horses, no matter how well you treat them, they can and do step on you for no obvious reason.

You don't hear many shooters talk about guns they hated, but I have owned several. One was a three-inch magnum, 12-gauge pump that I saved my lunch money to buy during a brief period when I considered myself a world-class waterfowler. The gun would indeed bring down the odd bird, but in the process it would also jar your cheekbones, loosen your teeth, and smash your head against the back of the blind. I've had a few pump guns that I shot respectably, both in the field and at trap and skeet, and I consider the pump about ideal as a duck and goose gun. But this particular pump was an abomination.

Being both cheap and stubborn, I tinkered with the beastly thing, combining all my knowledge of both gunsmithing and elementary physics. I put a two-pound steel rod in the magazine with the same satisfaction you get from kicking a flat tire. But if anything, the recoil was worse, not to mention that it made the gun even more clumsy to handle. I shortened the stock and fired one shell, and when my nose quit bleeding, I lengthened the stock. If you've ever been in the ring with a good counterpuncher, you know just how I felt.

Nobody I knew believed you could "double" a pump gun until they shot this one. Even my father, who never shot anything but some kind of pump and didn't know what recoil was, handed it back to me after two shots—one he did on purpose and the other the gun did for him.

I finally traded the gun and I hope whoever ended up with it dropped it overboard and let it drown. I wish I had—it would have been a satisfaction that money can't buy.

I've also had a few guns that I just couldn't shoot with any consistency, and a couple that I just couldn't shoot at all. I had one gun that I hated for no better reason than it was ugly; I couldn't wait to trade it off in spite of the fact that I had some of my best trap scores ever with it. One of the guns I could never shoot well was a Winchester Model 21 skeet gun. I bought it for upland shooting, but I couldn't even claim to be pathetic with it. Those were the days when I didn't know enough to realize that there is a certain *something* about certain guns that just doesn't make sense but is there nevertheless. I really never *liked* the gun for unexplainable reasons and so I just couldn't shoot it. I've had other 21s before and since that worked for me, but I've never been sorry that I got rid of that one.

Then there was the sleek little 28-gauge over-under that I absolutely loved. If you ever saw a gun that *looked* like it was destined to make its owner famous in woodcock or quail covers across the land, this was surely the one. When I first got that sweet little gun, I took it out to the skeet range with my usual

fair to poor results, but then I figured that I was a fair to poor skeet shot anyway; in the alders, I'd be a lightning strike!

Well, there was a lot of noise, but the lightning never struck twice in the same place. I think the gun was just too fast for me and I probably shot over or in front of everything, or below and behind, or somewhere; the gun always seemed to shoot where a bird wasn't. I couldn't bear to get rid of the gun, so I let one of my shooting buddies try it. He believes he was born to shoot that 28, so it's on what *he* calls "permanent loan."

There's a military adage—von Clausewitz maybe —that goes, "Never reinforce losses." And anyway, most of us are too stubborn to admit to a mistake, especially one that's as costly as a gun. It's taken me years to winnow out the guns I don't like; it has also cost me a lot of enjoyment since missing birds and turning in schoolgirl target scores is not my idea of a good time.

You can't ignore the aesthetics of the problem either. One friend spent years finding and then saving for a 20-gauge London "best" gun. I doubt if a more lovely side-by-side has ever been made. It had the classic understated elegance and lines that grace great museum sculptures, and it felt "alive" in that special way you really can't describe. Of course you can guess the problem. My friend just couldn't hit quail or doves or anything with this lovely bird gun. He asked me what I thought was wrong, and I told him, "The gun is simply too good for you." He was very disappointed with my answer but, as we all know, some days you're rained out.

I really don't have many regrets about selling or trading shotguns that weren't kind or obedient to me, their master; I know there are only very few around that I can shoot respectably, and I keep searching for them as religiously as a philosopher seeks the "truth."

A little-known fact is that guns are capable of jealousy. If you have one suitable quail gun and in a moment of misguided passion acquire another, neither one will provide that longed-for three-out-of-five average, day-in, day-out. Trap guns are even worse because they insist on being the one-and-only and thrive mightily on being pampered and bragged about.

Years ago I was attending the Grand American Trapshoot in Ohio and had the pleasure of watching a young man take his perfectly good trap gun and jam it in a trash barrel. His satisfaction was enormous and I envied his courage. I was watching a heroic act, a man ridding himself of a demon. I'd have traded it off, ending up with neither the great feeling of vindication, nor, according to past performances, any kind of break-even. Maybe used guns ought to come with a warning, something like "Caution! This gun cannot be relied on for high house two."

I see no point in keeping a gun you don't like. Life is too short, and so is hunting season. And as soon as I find how to trade guns without getting too badly hurt, or selling one for at least what you paid for it, I'll write it all down.

9

BREAKERS AND FIXERS

It is a well-known fact that the sportsmen of the world are divided into two very distinct groups—the Breakers and the Fixers. Being one of the former, I attract the latter like flies to garbage.

Fixers can be identified very easily. They carry jumper cables and a set of good tools in the car. They have a Swiss Army knife in their pocket, backed up by a key chain to which is attached a little set of screwdrivers, including a Phillips. Breakers carry duct tape and sometimes a pair of pliers. Fixers always have a flashlight that works and they can find it; the super-fixer carries extra batteries and a bulb—and a spare mantle for the camp gas lantern. A Breaker can rarely find his flashlight, and if he does, it is oozing a telltale green fluid.

The true Breaker doesn't have tools that are any good even if he could find them, and if he did, the Fixer who always shows up would disdain them anyway. I used to carry a few wrenches in my car only to discover that they were metric and my car needed whatever the opposite of metric is—the Fixer has them in his forty-pound tool box.

If you're at a fishing camp and one man is scowling and laying out an array of hot patches and glue sticks, and peering inside a pair of waders with a flashlight, while another man is sitting on the porch with a smile and a drink, you can bet that the Fixer is happily at work on the Breaker's problem.

Fixers always ask you, "How did it go today?" hoping you'll say something like "Not so good. The stripping guide came off my fly rod and the reel seat is starting to wobble." The nearest Fixer will have a small vise, winding thread that matches your rod, and varnish, and he will leap on the offending rod like a starving dog on a bone. When Fixers can't find a problem with your equipment, they'll walk around tightening the screws in the door hinges and sanding real or imaginary whiskers out of the canoe paddles. Being a kind soul, I mention right off that all my hooks seem to be dull and the nail knots lumpy; this will keep one Fixer busy for at least two evenings.

Gun Fixers are as comforting to me in hunting camp as a gastrointestinal specialist. At the minimum they'll run a swab through a fouled bore and check for looseness in things that ought to be tight. A scope off half-an-inch at 100 yards is just cause for a celebration, and a balky trigger is pure heaven. A high average gun Fixer will bring half a dozen hand-filed screwdrivers, two or three kinds of pliers, a plastic-head hammer, a few lubricants and cleaners, and possibly a choke gauge.

He will pick up your rifle and say "Bolt's a little sticky, mind if I look at it?" Before the hunt is over, he'll check every rifle in camp.

Every camp is sure to have a Fixer that you might call the Compleat Woodsman. If you break a bootlace, and someone always does, he has a spare pair. Dull knife? He has two stones: coarse and fine. No corkscrew? Not to worry. Lost the valve in your air mattress? Just happen to have an extra. He will be the only man in camp with a spare compass, waterproof matches, water purifying tablets, three kinds of bandages, and a magnifying glass to get the speck out of your eye. I know this is why he goes to hunting camp, just as I know why vultures circle a sick cow.

Even a man not normally identified as a Fixer can have his moment. As farfetched as it may seem, even I have had one or two moments, although I am normally on the opposing side. One time that looms large was when an Indian guide couldn't start the outboard motor in the middle of a big lake. After several moments of pure panic, I saw that the starter rope had broken, took off the motor housing, and fixed it. While not exactly a heart transplant, that deed has given me much pleasure to look back on over the years.

One Fixer in a camp of half a dozen or more sports is about right. Otherwise they get to quarreling over who ought to right which wrong, frequently at the risk of doing damage that no one can fix. One exception is a doctor. I have never seen a medical man volunteer to so much as remove a splinter. On the contrary. He will claim, although we all know otherwise, that his real field is gynecology or prenatal care, leaving the horse wrangler to have a go with a hoof pick. A veterinarian, used to working with dumb animals, is usually far more willing to take a look. Although I am not a real Fixer, I have always had a secret urge to heal, and I look on a good, deep cut or a minor sprain as a godsend! I actually took a couple of stitches on a friend, and I will follow him around forever; should he stumble and fall, I will swoop down like a hawk of mercy!

The truth, of course, is that I am a Breaker. I built a reputation by locking myself out of my car on several occasions and then kept my hand in, so to speak, by breaking rod tips so often that I almost sank to carrying a spare tip guide myself. Of course, I wouldn't have had any way to glue it on, but the temptation was there.

My father, who knew me all too well, would rather have left his good tools out in the rain than see one of them in my grubby little hands. He wouldn't even let me borrow his yardstick and carpenter's pencil when I was a grown man. I was at least thirty-five years old before he would let me go to the hardware store for nails or screws without giving me a note for the clerk. Even now as I try to remember which rings go first on my automatic duck gun, I can imagine him, looking down at me from the Great Workshop in the sky, shaking his head in puzzled wonder how few things have changed at all.

If you're at a fishing camp this summer, you may see a man trying to get two inches of laces to work in four eyelets on his wading shoes. He'll be wearing an old brown sweater buttoned up a bit askew, with pipe tobacco holes in it. Don't be afraid to come over and say hello. If you don't step on my rod, and if you have an extra pair of laces, I'll try to sprinkle sand in someone's reel for you.

10

WATCHING
OUT

Last fall I spent a day at the Mesa Verde Park in Colorado, an ancient place once inhabited by cliff dwellers. In the fine little museum run by the Park Service, the tranquil scenes in the dioramas of Indian life depict women weaving baskets, cooking, taking care of the children. The men are standing around staring into the wilderness, often with a dog at their side.

I overheard a lady remark how typical it was to see the women doing all the work while the men just lounged around doing nothing. The lady was wrong. Those ancient cliff dwellers weren't simply doing *nothing*—they were *watching out*.

Watching out is still a popular pastime in most of America; I believe it's deep in the masculine genes. What does a small boy do when he climbs a tall tree? He watches out! A grown man leaning against his tractor, seemingly doing nothing, is actually obeying the deep urge to watch out. Even a boy standing on a street corner or sitting on an apartment stair is doing what nature intended for men to do—watching out.

Men watching out together is common wherever you see a bridge with room to stand. It's almost a foregone conclusion that if one man is standing there looking over the landscape, another will be on the other side of the bridge doing the same thing. All they need is a dog to come along and join in. I don't believe anyone knows when man first taught dogs to watch out—there are a lot of links missing in our social history—but it may have been one of his more important and lasting contributions. A really well-run farm or country place has several dogs watching out, one at the head of the lane, one on or under the porch, and one rover covering the large gaps.

The urge to watch out is so strong that men prepare for it almost subconsciously. I can think of no other reason for those little ladders on the backs of vans and RVs than to offer us a little high ground when we feel the urge.

Our earliest painters showed us Indians watching from the rims of mesas and canyons, hands shading their eyes. The casual observer can be forgiven for thinking that they were watching out for buffalo or unfriendly warriors. The scholar or a student of watching out knows better; in fact, the appearance of buffalo or warriors can be an intrusion, breaking the rhythm of the art of watching. We've all seen pictures of men with vision, men like Daniel Boone or Kit Carson, peering off into the distant wilderness. Romantics or unthinking persons assume that these pioneers were looking Westward or searching the horizon for smoke, when in reality they were merely watching out.

Occasionally, but not often, a man watching out will be doing something else, like whittling, chewing a straw, smoking a pipe, or holding a stick. These activities, all secondary to watching out, can be attributed to the influence of women; the man is merely seeking to avoid the possibility of female criticism or confrontation. When a male child is old enough to understand, he will be taught to prepare himself for the day when it will be his turn to watch out. It's true that some boys don't take to it and would rather be working, but society has room for everyone and these boys can grow up to be useful as well.

Many anthropologists believe that men took to hunting and fishing as a relief from watching out. I have no doubt that this is true. A man who is superior at watching out is also superior in the field or on the stream; it is well known that at least 99 percent of a man's hunting or fishing time is spent watching out in one form or another, and that the periods of intense activity are both rare and infrequent.

Society has a way of coming full circle. If you look at the great revival in bow hunting, for example, you'll see a group of men who are trying to find yet another way of making watching out semi-legitimate. Fly fishing is another sporting pastime in which a man can simply watch out. The garlands of paraphernalia lend an air of seriousness that allows a fly fisherman to just stand there completely at peace, waving his rod now and then to perk up his circulation or break up a swarm of midges. Deer hunting, by far our most popular shooting sport, is, as you by now have guessed, almost pure watching out, punctuated every four or five years by a shot or the actual taking of a buck.

The obvious question that men dread most is, "What are you watching out *for*?"

You might as well ask someone, "Why are you fishing?", or hunting? Watching out is not a results-oriented thing, but it does allow the mind total freedom. I have no doubt that many great things were invented by men who were watching out—like the brick and the grape-colored worm, for example. What do you think I'm busy doing when I get my best ideas?

11

PRACTICE MAKES
ADEQUATE

As luck would have it, I have managed to spend a fair amount of time fishing around the country over the past few years. Whenever I ask my guides what is the biggest problem they have with clients, the answer is always the same: "They can't cast."

Translation: a lot of people who spend a lot of money on fishing trips literally can't throw a fly line with *any* accuracy for *any* distance. This is very puzzling, since the same person, if he played golf, would spend hours on the practice tee and take a few lessons every so often—even the professionals do that.

By knowing how to cast, the guides don't mean the ability to throw a line eighty feet and put the fly in a teacup. A perfectly satisfactory cast is forty to fifty feet, and if you can regularly come within ten or twelve inches of your "spot," you'll catch fish.

Throwing a long line, even under ideal conditions, is not easy. I know, because I'm still working and practicing. I also know that it's rarely, if ever, necessary. What *is* necessary is to practice. Even really fine casters practice *all the time*.

When I started fly fishing, I found an instructor through friends in the business and he and I went off to a lawn to work on my casting. After a full day, I was still terrible, but I was beginning to understand the process. All the while I marveled at Bill's easy expertise. He told me anyone could do what he did, if they also practiced a few minutes almost every day, which he did religiously. So I continued to practice and I enrolled in the Orvis School with my daughters, and then attended several other schools. I'm still not nearly as good as I'd like to be, or should be, but I can normally get the fly over fish.

Every religious or political nut wonders why everyone else doesn't believe what he believes, and I'm that way about fly fishing. I think it's just dumb to plunk yourself down on a fine piece of water and not be able to cope with it. I've seen this happen many times. I was at a very fine and expensive salmon camp a few years ago. There were ten fishermen in camp and only three were good casters. The rest depended on the guide to either do most of the casting, or to run the canoe too close to the salmon lies and hope that the fish didn't spook.

One man asked me to show his son-in-law the basics, since he'd never fished before. I tried but it was pretty hopeless. He worked at it, but like all first-timers he was trying too hard. Cast after cast settled on the water in a snarl of leader and line a few feet from the canoe. Just before lunch I told him we should go back to the dock and practice because it might be easier than casting from a boat.

"One more cast," he said, "and we'll quit." By pure luck and with a helpful gust of wind, his fly went out in a straight line for a full thirty feet and disappeared in a swirl. Forty-five very nervous and sweaty and instruction-filled minutes later, he landed his first salmon. It just happened to be a touch over forty pounds, which just happens to be the biggest salmon I've ever seen in a net. The Lord works in mysterious ways!

It's heartening to learn that last year was one of the most successful in the history of the tackle business, especially for fly fishing. A few of the biggest rod makers sold every rod they made, and this seems to be an ongoing trend. But I wonder how many newcomers will stay with fly fishing and how many will decide that they can't handle the casting because they won't take lessons and practice. It can be frustrating watching everyone else take fish. I've been there. But I like to practice and I do, even though my practice doesn't always make for perfect casting. My shooting experience is about the same, so I'm no stranger to disappointment, but at least I can get by in both disciplines, and that's a big improvement over where I was in the beginning.

If I were starting out again I'd do even more in the way of lessons and schools since I've developed a couple of faults that by now are so built in I really have to think about my casting when I should be just thinking about fishing; I ought to be doing more "where" than "how."

One of the advantages of a fishing school is that you can try a variety of rods and find an action that suits you. A fine caster can use just about any out-fit, but the rest of us will end up liking one type of rod better than another for starters. I tend to like a very powerful action, since I often throw too hard and the rod minimizes the result. This is part of being stronger than I am skillful, but that's one reason there are so many rod actions on the market. In general, today's tackle is simply magnificent. The technology and materials make fly casting easier for anyone; in fact, I'd go so far as to say that it's hard to find a rod that isn't pretty good no matter how little you pay for it.

The real pleasure in fly fishing doesn't start until you can take your casting as almost second nature. I suggest small goals to begin with. Forget about hauling or shooting line and work on a simple *accurate* overhead cast of about thirty feet. Time and practice will take care of the rest of it. Then you can fish in the true sense of the word and learn the niceties of working the wet fly or placing the dry, reading the water and really getting as involved in fishing as a heron is—which is why you're there in the first place.

A few years ago, my assigned salmon beat on Quebec's George River was a submerged rock ledge. Since I had a favoring wind and a strong belief that the salmon were lying a fair distance out of the river, I spent the morning double hauling and whatever else I could think of to get as much line out as possible. I never got a strike.

In the afternoon another guy had the same beat. I'd known him for years and to say that he was a marginal caster would be generous, but he *could* pinpoint the fly out thirty or so feet. I smugly wished him well.

At the end of the day he had six fine fish. Turns out the salmon were in close, and this guy carefully fished every square foot of water in a thirty-foot radius.

Someone once told me you'll catch ten fish at forty feet or less for every one you hook farther out. I believe that. I just have to ignore the little devil that sometimes sits on my shoulder and whispers, "You've got a nice following breeze..."

12

GIVING
THANKS

Like most of us, I give thanks a lot, and I should. Most of my thanksgiving is in response to the unexpected, maybe even the undeserved. I'm thankful, for example, that I found—at long last—the box that holds most of my streamer flies. And I'm thankful that some genius designers have made rods even I can cast with, and that at least a few trout are not all that fussy about a drag-free float.

There's a frequent nod of gratitude at the call of "dead bird" when I know I didn't get anywhere near enough to deserve it. When the better shots don't show up for the 28-gauge event, I breathe a silent sigh of relief. Actually, just remembering my rain jacket or discovering a forgotten pair of shooting glasses in the trunk of my car is cause for reserved celebration.

Of course I'm grateful for making a clean double on drakes in front of an audience; having the pup really "sit" and "stay" when I'm showing her off; discovering that I really do shoot a bit better with the new gun;

guessing which fork in the dirt road leads to camp; remembering to sign my duck stamp *before* the warden checks me out (four nods!).

A special thanks, and a smile, is in order for missing a woodcock that you deep down really didn't want, or when the dog brings back your grouse while the guide is teasing you about being too pokey with the gun. And we all must be thankful for seeing fresh pheasant tracks in the snow, or having the big tom answer our owl hooter.

There is another level of thanksgiving that is more personal, more individualized. I'm thankful that my professional life has allowed me to spend time doing the things I like with people I like who are better than average at their chosen craft. I have been able to fish a lot with Lee Wulff and Ed Zern and a few others you might recognize—not at their level, but at least in the same rivers. I have been out-shot by Rudy Etchen and Homer Clark and Billy Perdue, to name the more familiar of dozens. I've been privileged to spend time afield with the likes of Abbett, Maass, Kuhn, Cohleach, and Hennessey, and learn about their approaches to outdoor art. I've learned a lot from all of these friends. I did so *without* becoming a better fisherman, shot, or art critic, but that's not what's really important.

I am especially delighted to give thanks for being able to chat, once a month, with people more like me. People who write to tell me about their dogs, guns, friends, the good days and the bad. My people agree, disagree, or see things in another way. They believe, rightly, that if I can talk to them, they can talk back. It's deeply satisfying to get a note that says "...I've been thinking about what you've said..."

I'm thankful that there are so many places I haven't fished and so many places I haven't hunted. I haven't lost the small boy wonder that comes from staring at maps, or the tingle of the explorer's anticipation. The glisten of starlight on a river still somehow overpowers the fact that in another direction I can too often see the glare of the city lights. Civilization is a harsh fact, but with a little imagination we dreamers can deal with it. As long as the fish don't know that the rumble is a truck or a train, not thunder, I can pretend as well; the choice between the dream and the reality is still an easy one.

I'm thankful I can still see the places I'm so fond of the way they once were. I can close my eyes and hear the canvasbacks circling over a Chesapeake tidewater creek, pretending the high-rise isn't there. My old woodcock covers with their stands of birches and poplar are still the orange-yellow of autumn, not brick. I cover in minutes the miles I once trudged through a swamp, but I can still see my first deer standing there by the edge of a clearing now paved. And there is always a very clear vision of the young man who was my father, so pleased because for once I had done something right, asking me if I'd remembered my knife, and laughing when I shook my head.

Then there are other pictures, common but priceless, the kind that need no words other than giving thanks to life itself. Holding a very ordinary shotgun lets me remember the other hands that once held it and what it meant to both of us when the gun was given to me. Putting a worm on my grandson's hook lets me show him, I hope, how easily so many little fears can be faced head-on. The night calls of the geese still tug my heart, and hearing the hunting owl still stirs my mind.

I'm especially thankful to have seen those special places I hardly dared dream about as a youngster, and for the pleasure of hearing birds flush, seeing fish rise and deer run, leaving them undisturbed so they will be there when I turn the page tomorrow.

13

THE

DOG MAN

A friend of mine, or rather his springer spaniel, just had a litter of pups. Knowing that I'm dogless at the moment, he tested me rather severely by handing me a tiny brown-and-white male. The pup closed his eyes and put his head on my shoulder and went to sleep.

I closed my eyes too for a minute and tried to remember all the pups I've held—and took home—where each quickly voted himself or herself chief executive officer, and took over the treasury, and made severe adjustments in my vacation schedule.

But not this time. I put the pup back on the ground and watched with a great deal of satisfaction as he went back to work decimating the pachysandra bed. My own pachysandra is almost back to where it was twenty years ago, but then it's a pretty tenacious plant.

Back in my office I looked around and saw so many dog things hanging here and there that I haven't looked at in years. Training dummies, collars, leashes, flushing whips, bells, combs, and brushes—and flea spray and blank cartridge pistols. Here and there stuck on an old picture frame or hung from a lampshade are a few ribbons from Senior Puppy stakes and intermediate trials and even an old cigarette box won by one of my English setters.

The setter was a female orange Belton, handsome to a fault and with all the capriciousness her sex is notorious for. She was stubborn, vain, jealous, and temperamental, and a classic worker when it suited her, which wasn't often. I once lost a quail over a creek I couldn't cross when she refused to go get it, so I spent an inordinate amount of time stumbling along with lessons from books, training her—force breaking, really—to retrieve. To my complete amazement she became virtually perfect at it. Not only did she almost never lose a bird; each one was held with classic form, delivered to hand, and released only when I tapped her gently under her lovely chin.

Overwhelmed with success and filled with *hubris* at my new found genius as a dog trainer, I decided that a brace of setters was mandatory. No doubt I was living in some dream world populated by visions of the hunt master behind a brace of classic pointing dogs—himself, immaculate in khaki shirt and tie, sporting a good English double. Of course, with the possible exception of the shirt and tie, none of the above became reality.

The addition to my "kennel" was a blue-blooded tricolor named Ben, out of a long line of champion Pennsylvania grouse dogs. Orchard Valley and Sam L's Rebel, if memory serves. This male exhibited all the capriciousness his sex is notorious for; he was stubborn, vain, know-it-all, reckless, and bold. But underneath there was a fine dog, a true birdy hunter, *if* you had winged heels and could find him. So it was back to the training books and hundreds of yards of check cords, choke collars, and finally a log chain that must have outweighed him by five pounds. What the log chain did, in the main, was increase his leg muscles and stamina, and I can still see it throwing sparks over the rocks in one of my favorite bird coverts as its jangle faded away into the mysterious beyond. On one of these expeditions, Ben lost a large part of a front foot to a fox trap. My vet was dubious about whether or not he'd get back to normal, while I, callously, thought, *It's an ill wind that blows nobody good*...He may not have been quite as fast on three and a half legs as he was on four, but you needed a stop watch to prove it.

I've had many other adventures with bird dogs, including the one that began when I came home from a Ducks Unlimited dinner with a Labrador puppy. At the moment someone said, "I now pronounce you man and Labrador," my life changed dramatically. New books, new wardrobe, new tools, some shouting, and some cajoling, but all worth it.

Tip was a born lady and if you treated her as her station required, she would do as asked. All she insisted on was that the task be carefully explained. I never could get her to heel properly, probably because she thought it beneath her. And it was always difficult to get her to honor another dog's retrieve when she thought she could get the job done quicker and better.

It's odd how you remember the little bents that special dogs leave you with. Tippy had two that always (almost always) charmed me. She loved to sleep late and we argued a lot about getting up before dawn. She also had an insatiable love for chocolate candy, and over the years she pretty well trashed the car seats looking for my candy stash.

A man without a dog doesn't have to worry about lugging log chains, or remembering to stick a Hershey bar in his duck coat. He doesn't have to steel himself against the cries of woe from the dog left behind in the kennel, or get up in the middle of the night when he hears chewing. He doesn't have to walk outside on a rainy night, or wonder why the full moon has to be barked at. He doesn't have to pray for straightaway shots, flail his arms when opening the kitchen door to protect his clothes, or fish tennis balls out from under the stove.

On the other hand, a dogless man's heart doesn't beat as fast when he steps into a bird field, or when he pulls into his driveway. Mine still beats fast, running to keep pace with the hope and memories of this time of the year.

14

Fear of
Snoring

When a group of men gather on the first evening
of a trip, they introduce themselves, chat about the
weather, and ask about hometowns, other trips, and
the like. It may sound like small talk, but in reality it
disguises each sport's most deeply rooted fear—is he
going to have to room with someone who snores?

Water conditions, game populations, the quality of the food, or the severity of the weather pale
beside the enormous dread of spending a night staring
at the ceiling or the sky while making up your mind
whether or not to poke a sleeping 200-pound neighbor
with a stick in order to gain a minute or two of quiet
before he starts in again.

There are a lot of theories as to why men make
war, commit murder, or use weighted nymphs with fluo-
rescent bobbers and call it fly fishing. I'm not nearly as
interested in all that as I am in a cure for snoring. There
will be a Nobel Prize in the offing for the genius who

can return quiet to the sleeping hours, unless I have totally misconstrued the meaning of "benefit for all mankind."

I was astounded to discover that the proprietor of one hunting camp—the only one I know of—had made a great effort to soundproof the walls between rooms. He was making a big thing about it when I pointed out that each area had three or four beds and what if I had the misfortune to be forced to share a room with someone as internationally famous for spreading insomnia as, say, Ed Zern? He had no answer, of course, because there is no legal, socially acceptable answer.

Statistically, in a room of four there is at least one Zern, or his near equal. And in my experience they are hard to spot. In general I tend to avoid roommates that exceed the normal height-for-weight charts by a large margin. I also shun heavy smokers and ex-boxers or football players, because they have broken noses and *always* snore. Men who are balding tend to snore a lot also, though I can't imagine why. Anyone can snore at times—even I have been accused, mistakenly, of course. Unfortunately, there are no hard and fast rules, and a man who isn't really a snorer can suddenly come into his own and keep as many as three rooms awake in a hunting or fishing camp. Russian roulette is what we're talking about—sooner or later, at one camp or another, you have to lose.

For obvious reasons, I have spent a lot of time discussing the subject with Zern. Ed believes that snoring is actually a social asset that goes back to the cave dweller, when, Ed claims, the greatest snorer was revered as one who kept dangerous animals at a safe distance through the night. I have no doubt that Ed can do this, but there have been many nights when I would have welcomed a choice. I told Ed that I saw some merit in his theory, but that I would like the chance to sleep on it. Zern merely smiled; I thought the remark deserved a little more recognition.

If you take a hundred men, all certified as snorers by witnesses with signed affidavits, ninety-nine of them would deny it. I simply don't understand this. If I snored, I would be honest enough to admit it.

How a woman can live with a man like that, share the same room, the same bed, says something about consortium that I don't understand. No doubt it is the same defensive mechanism that makes a snake impervious to its own venom.

I came back from a woodcock hunt in Maine a few years ago totally exhausted from the nocturnal oratorios of my roommate. My eyes were mere slits from fatigue and my hands trembled so much from exhaustion that I had to take my evening Ovaltine through a straw. I couldn't wait to ask his wife what her secret was. Ear plugs, sleeping drops, self-hypnosis—there had to be something, short of sleeping all day and staying up all night. I was shocked, not at the fact that *he* denied snoring, his morning sore throat evidence to the contrary, but that *she* denied it as well.

"Jay doesn't snore, absolutely not, never," she told me. I started to tell her that the second night in camp, I put my shotgun in the hall for fear that the vibration might loosen the screws in the sideplates, but realized my exhortations would have been useless. I can only marvel that we have not yet been reduced through natural selection to the survival of only the stone deaf.

My normal escape mechanism in camp is to try to get to sleep before the show starts. I have been known to take to my bed halfway through supper in hopes of getting in a couple of hours of sleep, but this only works if the bedroom is a fair distance away from the dining room. Moving the bed is fine, provided you don't move it out of the frying pan into the fire. I tried this at a dove camp last year and was awakened by a quartet of offenders of such varying pitch and rhythm that I simply gave up and spent the night trying to remember the psalm about being forsaken.

Of course, the ideal camp setup would be individual, soundproof rooms. But of course, we're not going to find such a camp. The closest I've come was having my own private cabin at a fishing camp. Actually, the cabin was being used as a tool locker until I discovered it had a bunk bed and a mattress. It was smelly, with the odd mouse and some other creatures about, but they didn't snore.

Lest you think I'm one of those people who have the ears of a bat, let me assure you that I'd still be wearing my hearing aid If I hadn't dropped it in the Madison River and I'd rather not say how.

I wish I had a functional answer, a solution we could all use in self-defense. An electronic collar like they sell for barking dogs would work except I don't think I want to be the first one to suggest it. I've tried earplugs, but they always fall out when I need them most, or else I forget they're there until everybody starts shouting at me, or I sleep through the alarm and miss my pancakes and sausage.

I'm tired of having to get my sleep in duck blinds, deer stands, or curled up in the bilge. I want to close my eyes, listen to the soft sounds of the night, and dream of five-pound rainbows and ten-point bucks—not lie there wide awake, wondering why there isn't another commandment—"Thou shalt not snore!"

15

THE COVER
OF DARKNESS

I don't care much for fly fishing at night. Something evil happens to my casting and wading, and I worry about what might go wrong. When the bats come out, I'm ready to call it a day.

I got talked into a late-night fishing expedition some years ago on the usual promise of giant trout. I still believe these stories, partly because I want to and partly because I owe it to the tradition that says if you want giant trout, you must seek them under the cover of darkness. An old friend whom I rarely see swore he'd been saving the pool for me. So at eleven o'clock, in full darkness, I eased into the water and waded out, hoping I was far enough from the bank to keep my fly out of the brush but not so far that the next step might be my last one on earth. My friend did say that the water ran a bit deep toward the middle; I also noted that my friend is six feet, six inches tall, and I am not. Then he gave me the clincher: "Gene?" he called. "Okay so far," I answered. "Keep an eye out for boats," he called back. "What boats?" I asked. "Some guides have been running camps upriver and they come back about this time."

I couldn't see the end of my fly rod in the dark and I could barely hear the distant thunder because of years of shooting. But experience has taught me that I

am a magnet for weird incidents like being run over in the dark by a drift boat. They can't see me and I can't see them; perfect, just perfect.

"No problem," I shouted, having already made up my mind to wade back to shore, smoke my pipe, and wait this whole absurdity out.

And that's just what I did. I sat there and listened to the night sounds of the river which, unfortunately, included whoops of near hysteria from my friend as he hooked half a dozen large-as-advertised trout. The guide boats never showed up, but I had mixed emotions about that. I was once run over by a canoe and it would have been interesting to see things from a different angle, so to speak.

Bass fishing at night is something entirely different. For one thing, and a big one it is, you're in a boat. And I don't have any problems with a casting rod after dark. In fact, I'd rather cast a plug for bass under starlight than during the day; there are fewer people to disturb you and the fishing is often better and more gently paced in the company of swallows, bats, and owls.

I don't know why, but the topwater strike of a bass at night always seems louder and more thrilling. Part of it is because you concentrate on the path of the lure more in the dark and depend on hearing rather than sight. And a bass that you only *hear* and lose has to be a couple of pounds larger than one you *see* and lose.

Nights are busier than they used to be. The lights of jetliners and globe-circling satellites stitch across the skies, and sitting here casting a old wooden plug seems out of phase with the real world. I might as well be drawing stick figures on a cave wall while the computers take the temperatures of the stars. A loud *splat* brings me back to earth as my rattling plug gets thrown from the jaw of a fish. I estimate its weight conservatively at well over six pounds, after factoring in the romance of the darkness. Maybe seven pounds.

Since man is not a nocturnal animal, familiar objects tend to take on an altered state after dark. A tree that by day is a sheltering refuge offering shade and a place to ease the wind and rest the eyes can, by night, become a ghoulish hand reaching into a dark sky. A brook that calms by day turns dark and ominous in the night. The known and the unknown change places.

I have on several occasions legally shot ducks at night in Great Britain. The best kind of night is a half or better moon behind a scrim of clouds giving a background with just enough light to turn the birds into visible shadows. The usual wariness is gone and the ducks swing into the wind and drop down like stones. The gunner shifts his senses from eyes to ears and listens for the wing noise. I must admit that it violates my sense of fair play and takes away the matching of wits that is so much a part of what I like about waterfowling—the decoys, the calling, the messing with the "perfect" blind, the mounting thrill as a long line of birds weaves through the sky toward you, in that tense immobilizing time of "will they or won't they?"

The dark may be a great comfort for many whose edge of survival is more sharply honed than ours. The trout and the elk alike need a nearby place of darkness in order to feel secure, and the owl needs a time to hunt. But the setting of the sun for me is a silent ticking of the clock. I hear a bass jump in the pond and imagine the fate of a frog that trusted the dark. I think for a minute about getting the casting rod but decide against it. The dog whimpers and I tease it by asking, "Afraid of the dark?" An owl answers for both of us and whatever else might be listening. The dog starts to run toward the lights of home, and for the same reasons, so do I.

16

IN MY
OPINION

Interesting ideas that defy proof appeal to me, because facts have a way of strangling speculation and pestering us daydreamers. I have longed to scratch some of my itches in public, so here they are. You may not itch in exactly the same places, but hear me out. Please.

There seems to be a current fad that is, like a lot of fads, foolishly logical—the left-handed operation of a fly reel. "Why are you doing this the awkward way?" the sensible, right-handed angler asks before forcing you to listen to a tedious explanation about how fighting a trout of a pound or so requires the mightier of your appendages. Nonsense. If a twenty-inch rainbow (you should be so lucky) exhausts you, take up something less strenuous like free form verse.

The Labrador retriever is, arguably, the most perfect example of the kindness and compassion of the Almighty. Eve wasn't bad either, mind you, but just think about it...

The most satisfying way to catch bass is on a topwater plug. Least satisfying is the common worm rig.

Nymphing for trout with a bobber (strike indicator indeed!) has little to do with real fly fishing; it is, unfortunately, quite effective, but so are explosives and electric shockers.

Bureaucratic nitwittery has finally enacted a series of laws in every state I know of that seem to be specifically designed to totally discourage youngsters from ever taking up hunting. Read the laws in your state and imagine yourself being twelve or so. Add up the hours and the costs and the bother, divide by enthusiasm, and subtract a young man or woman, just when we need them more than ever.

Why have hunters and fishermen gone so deeply on the defensive as to resort to wimpy phrases like "harvest," or worse, "reduce to possession"? Would a Marine DI urge his troops to "harvest the enemy"? Are we retreating to the dark ages when piano legs were referred to as "limbs" and death was couched in a myriad of circumlocutions that didn't make the matter any less realistic or irreversible?

Is the current proliferation of state stamps, at extra costs, another bleeding of the sportsman? In many cases I suspect it is. Does your pheasant stamp money really go for pheasants, or should we remain skeptical? Is it too much to ask our public servants to tell us where our money really goes? It might make for amusing reading at worst; at best it might provoke some of us to ask some harder questions.

The wild turkey is our most overrated game bird. Other than giving us a spring hunting season and the chance to fool with a variety of calls and patterns of camouflage overalls, what have we got? The next most overrated bird is the Canada goose. Most underrated are the pintail and the sandhill crane. Just my personal opinion, of course.

"Hill's Law" says: "The surest way to find something you've lost is to replace it with something new." Another is that "One size doesn't fit all." An increasing number of clothing makers don't know their XLs from their Ss.

The best all-around shotgun shell is a No. 7½. Number 7s are even better, but only all of Europe and Great Britain know that. The 3-inch, 20-gauge shell is only really functional for those who like recoil. And since you asked, I don't know why they make a one-ounce load for the 28-gauge either.

The best all-around freshwater rod is an eight-footer for a seven-weight line. No saltwater fly rod should be less than nine feet for a nine line; if you only had one rod, a ten weight would be even better. These are the "12-gauges" of fly fishing; they will get the job done under almost every condition.

The best all-purpose dry fly is the Adams. The best all-purpose streamer is the Grey Ghost, and the best wet fly is the Hare's Ear. Hill has spoken!

The best all-around North American rifle caliber is the .270. I will admit to owning some others, but except for a few really heavy calibers, I don't know why—maybe because I wanted them.

The best shot is the one you make after your buddy has missed it twice.

The best deer is your first one. The next best is the first one you helped someone else get.

I hope you haven't forgotten how much fun it is to fish with live bait. It gives you a very special feeling about the world "down there," and it has a nice slow, reflective pace to it—primitive and strong and honest.

Pound for pound, saltwater fish fight harder than freshwater fish. No, I can't prove it and I don't know why; I just know it's true.

The perfect two-barrel choke borings for virtually all bird hunting are light improved-cylinder and tight-modified. Trust me! Not bad for a duck gun either in these days of steel shot. For a single barrel gun—improved-cylinder.

The excessive noise from short-barreled shotguns and rifles outweighs any imagined or hoped-for theoretical advantage if you expect to shoot more than one shot—or even ten. Short barrels are a delusion based on a number of false premises. If you don't believe me, ask someone who uses them, but you'll have to shout.

In closing, I urge you not to take anybody's word for anything, including mine, unless you want to, except for what I said about the Labrador. I believe the Lord made the earth round so retrievers wouldn't fall off the edge. Just my opinion, of course.

17

THE

FREE THINKERS

I was judging a field trial a couple of years ago and one of the dogs, a nice looking black Labrador, caught my eye. I have a weakness for lady Labs with style and an air of independence, and this one had both. She all but ignored her handler and left the impression that if it wasn't for him, she could really go places.

A co-judge noted my interest and nudged me. "She really doesn't like her handler," he said. "He's done something to upset her and she's letting him know."

Ladies have been known to do things like that, I thought, *and good for her.* Anyway, this dog, whose name was Annie, turned in quite an outstanding performance in every series, proving that my first impression was right, which it often is not. Her *I'll show you* attitude reminded me of other free spirits that I got to know very well.

The reasons are not important, but a friend arrived one day carrying a wire-haired pointing Griffon puppy. With a little ceremony, he put the dog in my arms and pronounced us "man and dog," sort of. *Okay, I thought, plenty of room in the kennel; what's one more dog? and he'll be an interesting change from the Labs.*

Like any dog nut, I played with George, bought him squeaky toys, gave him special treats, and did my best to make him feel at home. I finally realized that for some reason George simply didn't like me. He loved the girls and helped coach their high school cross-country team, but whenever I asked him to go for a walk to find a bird or a rabbit, he'd retreat to his lounge chair in the garage and say he was too tired or too busy and pretend to sleep or stare into the middle distance.

At first I was totally puzzled. I couldn't, and still can't, imagine how I'd hurt George's feelings. Of course, there's no reason why every dog has to like me because I give him or her room and board. A lot of people who don't like each other are under the same roof; why not dogs? But after a while I gave up on George. We were civil and exchanged nods when our paths crossed, but that's as far as it went. He did mellow a bit in time, and after he finally passed on I kept his brown chair in the garage; the sight of it often made me both sad and humble. What mysterious thing lay behind those soft brown eyes? Where had I failed? I'll never know.

Josephine, a matronly lady disguised as a black Labrador, liked me a lot. In fact she rather indulged me in her role as resident Queen and a dog who would have absolutely nothing to do with any training whatsoever. For reasons of her own, probably dietary, she was always prompt to appear when I called, but if she saw that it was a summons to chase dummies or some other such rowdiness, she'd have none of it. Yet she enjoyed watching the other dogs in training and she frequently barked and jumped around as if applauding or giving encouragement for a job well done. When the rest of us had gone away, she'd often slip into the pond like an overweight lady and enjoy a swim, paddling along with the members of a goose family.

Most days Jo would walk up the lane and wait for the school bus. In the fall, she'd stop and graze on the odd fallen apple, and if she heard the bus she'd rush along carrying her goody like a jewel, dropping it by the mailbox when the bus stopped so she could smile at the girls.

Jo spent much of her waking hours consumed by our mole problem. She had a peculiar way of holding her head, almost cocked like a robin, listening for underground goings-on. Suddenly she'd burst into a frenzy of digging and when no mole was found, she'd stand there looking plainly disappointed. Then after a while I'd see her poised over another run with unflagging determination.

Across the road from the head of the lane a neighbor with no tolerance for moles in his lawn was dousing the runs with poison and I guess Jo must have heard some underground squalling and gone over to investigate. Anyway, she dug up her one and only mole. The neighbor's wife called and said my dog was rolling around on her lawn and I ought to come up and take care of it. The poison had already coursed through her system, but Josephine knew I was there and thumped her tail gently as becoming a lady, slightly apologetic and in unseemly distress. I held her head and told her what I hoped she wanted to hear, then picked her up and carried her down the lane, past the fallen fruit and the red and yellow leaves. I stopped and put an apple in my pocket and found a place in the yard in a quiet spot past the pond where, for some reason, the moles never went.

I find that I miss the free thinkers when they leave. To be honest, a lot of my closest friends are and have been what you might charitably call free spirits. Ed Zern was one I spent a lot of time with, and when I once named a puppy after him, he was pleased no end. I trained Ed, the dog, enough to compete in some puppy trials where he caught the eye of a professional with a wealthy patron and I reluctantly sold the dog.

I called Zern and told him his namesake was on his way to Minnesota and was destined to make the name Zern famous.

"Did Ed exit laughing?" Zern asked.

"No, but I will," I said, and hung up before he could top me.

18

BLIND

SPOT

There was a time in my life when I was a *duck hunter*, fully dedicated to 3-inch magnums, full-choke shotguns, Labrador retrievers, and D.U. dinners in three or four states. When I wasn't doing that kind of honest work, I was shooting trap in training for the waterfowl season.

My local gunning ran from Barnegat Bay in New Jersey to the Eastern Shore of Maryland, and once a year I managed a visit to some mecca like Arkansas or Louisiana with my fellow pilgrims. But as great as those places can be, they wouldn't be my first choice if I had my pick of where to go for opening day.

My idea of a great place to hunt ducks has a heavy touch of the primitive, the rough edges of heaven and earth, where the outdoors is a sort of chaotic state. That's the great Delta Marsh in Manitoba. To me, that's what duck hunting is all about. A zillion acres of wet stuff which has been left alone by man. A place with almost no people; a place with two seasons, summer and duck.

During the years I celebrated opening day on this marsh I existed happily on the same breakfast of foods I haven't eaten in years: homemade sausage, ham, pork chops, oatmeal, eggs, two or three kinds of pie, biscuits, and pancakes. The last cup of coffee was always fired up with a slight touch of cheap blackberry schnapps. We raised our mugs to each other in a sincere and silent toast and left for the marsh.

No motors were allowed on the lake and no permanent blinds, either. We started fresh every day, picking this cove or that bay according to the wind. We loaded the boat by the cold light of the stars and bent to the oars. I liked to row and took a childish pride in seeing my wake as straight as a plumb line.

By first light our blind didn't look too bad. We were stuck deep in a pod of high phragmite grass which we'd folded back for a few lines of sight to the decoys. Ducks had been buzzing like bees as long as we'd been there, and we were just watching. This was what we came for and we were in no hurry to limit out.

A hundred ducks were swimming and feeding in the decoys. My favorite duck shot is a long crossing or incoming bird, never one with wings set and feet stretched out like orange bumpers, and I liked to wait for a big green-head drake or a bull pintail to come in off to one side. I felt that I knew to the foot what I could do with my old full-and-full Winchester and a load of heavy 5s, and I wasn't often wrong.

My partner and I stopped with five drakes apiece, short of the limit but enough to more than justify the day. The Indian guide rowed us back to the truck (I'm not sure I could have found it by myself) and we took a long dirt-road detour back to the camp, steeping ourselves in the cruel and beautiful grandeur of the prairie, chatting about how it must have been, not all that long ago, when uncounted buffalo lived here and the hunters were Indians and wolves.

Back at the camp I headed for a nap. As usual, the night before opening day had been close to sleepless. The same crowd of men who saw each other every week were acting like this was a twenty-fifth reunion. The ringleader was an ex-colonel in a Scottish regiment who always played the pipes sharply at midnight. If you weren't up, you got up and joined the march around and through the camp. The last piece played was always *Will Ye Nae Come Back Again*, which has always struck me as a profound and wonderful thing to listen to, especially with wind keening in from the north. When the piper finished we all trudged off to bed, but the music lingered long into the night for me; it had awakened some ancient ancestral ghost that refused to go to sleep.

There was a nice beach not far from camp where I liked to think I was walking off the Dutch apple pie à la mode. Long strings of ducks and shorebirds flew in every direction, dropping down from the sky like confetti on the wind. The hand of man touched very lightly here, and it was easy to believe "that it was ever thus and will be so forever."

Like every other camp, this one had its old pictures. Plunked down here, close to the middle of nowhere, were the likes of the Hemingways, Clark

Gables, and a scattering of other "names," as well as ordinary hunters. But they were all duckers. No one was there because of anything but the hunting; this was just a plain and simple duck camp. "Plain" may even flatter it a little.

I hear it's gone now. Deaths, quarrels, and neglect left it helpless. But I'm not that homesick for the camp or even the hunting—it's the time I weep for; how I *felt* about being where I was and doing what I was doing. This was one place where I was truly happy. How lucky I am to still hear the groan of the lopsided oarlocks and the tinkle of crystal-thin ice breaking at the bow and see the sky alive with ducks beyond counting. I remember thinking that nothing here should ever change. And it shouldn't have. But it does.

19

READING
WATER

I've always been intrigued with the idea of "reading water." Few anglers are truly skilled in this most refined of the fishing arts, and that's perfectly understandable. After all, you're dealing with a "living fluid" that flows through and over terrain that changes constantly and requires an understanding of water color, temperature, oxygen content, opacity, and the other ingredients that combine to make vital trout or salmon lies.

I remember fishing a salmon river for the first time and being too stubborn to ask the guide exactly where the fish might hold. Being a good part Scot, he was just as stubborn about answering my unasked questions. Finally I said something about this being a lovely stretch of water and he replied, "Indeed, unless you're a fish," and proceeded to move me about twenty yards and give me a lecture about the topography of the river bottom and how to identify the best lies. I've since learned a little about reading water and a lot about not being too hard-headed to ask about it.

I have a friend who is an expert at reading "pocket" water and fishing it with deadly little probing casts to this rock or that. But put him on big water and he's hopeless. I'm the opposite. I don't enjoy dropping a fly here and there like a seamstress doing embroidery. I prefer long, sweeping casts, acting under the delusion that the farther away the fish are, the bigger and more plentiful they must be. On the other hand, the real expert will do well on any kind of water because he listens to what the water tells him. It's part instinct, part knowledge, and part experience; and it's a lot rarer than you might believe. Many of us do well on a stretch of water that's local and familiar and delude ourselves that we're quite canny. But on new water, we lean pretty hard on lady luck, and she can be very fickle indeed.

Of course, even when you *are* "on," it's one thing to know that fish are under this bank or behind that rock, and another to do something about it. How the fly is presented is part of reading water and often one of the most difficult techniques. There are places where you just can't properly put a fly and places where you have to be very creative. But that's the fun, or frustration, of reading water, or trying to.

There are days when I like to experiment, and I take great pleasure in catching one or two fish in a less than conventional manner. Occasionally something wonderful happens and you have that euphoria of brilliance until you try the same technique another time and nothing happens. I once fished a huge salmon pool with two friends. Fish were rolling out in the middle, but other than a couple of little pecking hits, nothing rose but our frustration. No one knew a lot about the pool and our reaction to the situation was to change flies, the last refuge of the ignorant.

Finally I remembered a similar situation on another big river and changed (secretly, I will admit now) from a long leader and floating line to a three-foot leader and sink tip line. Immediately I was into fish. I hooked and released three fine salmon and modestly refused to discuss much about it except to credit my fly, a big Monro Killer. I could hardly wait for the next day, but I did sleep the restful sleep of the angler who has found *the* secret; nothing calms the nerves like a sure thing!

The pool was again alive with salmon the next morning, and I smoked my pipe while my companions fished fly after fly, with no results. Finally it was my turn and I was almost a little embarrassed to start casting. And as we all know, there is nothing so sweet as succeeding where your friends fail. But how sweet it was for them to watch me do absolutely nothing with those fish except reflect on yet another of the mysteries of salmon fishing. To this day I can't figure it out, but something had changed. Maybe the fish were just a little less "fresh," or the size of the fly was wrong for the light conditions, but none of us took another fish from that pool. I did have the satisfaction of reading it right, until the page was turned.

Once in a while I hit water that I have no idea how to fish, and end up tortured by the notion that if so-and-so were here, he'd know what to do. Worse is to think you've got it figured out, only to have someone who does know the water put you in places that are totally different than the ones you thought looked the most likely.

I tend to be a bit careless when it comes to being really good at knowing the secrets of a stream. I will even admit to fishing water that I know is unlikely to hold much because it's convenient, or I just like the way it moves. Sometimes the good water is too hard to fish or too difficult to get at, and I can talk myself into "skipping pages" the way I might leaf through a book that I started but lost interest in.

Like most of us, I go fishing for different reasons at different times. But this doesn't detract from my belief that reading water is about the highest level of accomplishment a fisherman can aspire to. It requires a nice blend of science and wishful thinking, and an ability to marry what you can't see and what you can. The real reader of moving water is not a visitor who stands on the porch and shouts "Is anybody home?" He's a habitue, one who peeks through the windows into the kitchen and the living room and knows if anyone is home, even when the shades are drawn. He may not be a practitioner of the black arts, but he does catch more fish.

20

Conspicuous Consumption

"Give someone a fish and that person will eat for a day. Teach someone to fish and that person will eat for a lifetime."

I saw this little homily embroidered on a pillow in the Orvis catalog, and it has been rattling around in my head ever since.

Never mind "catch and release," because that avoids the point. So does *eating* in the everyday sense; but since "eat" is the crux of this, I looked it up in my ten-pound dictionary. One of the definitions, after those you'd expect, is: "to devour, to consume, to feed destructively..." Now that's more like it!

I have taught a few people the rudiments of fly casting, which is almost all I know, and during the course of my "instruction," they have had occasion to drift through my office where it is an unavoidable fact that I have a lot of fishing stuff lying around.

"Surely you don't need all that?" they always say. I was once innocent and naive myself, so I just smile.

David is a typical newcomer to fly fishing. He sees himself nattily outfitted in waders, vest, and tweed hat, and equipped with a few pleasing trinkets—like a handmade wooden net, forceps, clippers, etc. He has gone for a five- or six-weight rod in the honest belief that this will do for the local trout, the odd weekend on the Little Placid. And so it will. Until he begins to *consume*.

There isn't any real order to the beginning of this feast, but it's common to first pick up a few good books, get some catalogs, subscribe to a couple of magazines, maybe even rent a video on steelhead or tarpon— just out of curiosity, mind you.

By now David has learned to do a decent roll cast and he can throw fifty feet of line close to where he wants to put the fly. He begins to seek the company of like-minded sportsmen, which dictates a little budget juggling for membership in a club. His wife, who is also an innocent, encourages this, "David's taken up fishing," she tells her buddies. "I'm so glad he has a nice outdoor hobby." She will learn that you can eat words.

Once in the club, David finds out that what the catalogs and magazines have said is true—one rod is not enough. He explains this to the Chief Financial Officer and she says she can understand that breakage can happen and she can see that some waters are wider and deeper than others, which means more distance, etc., etc. At this point David does not get into the details of extra reels, lines, spools, and flies at three-something apiece. Both David and his wife have passed GO and many angling shops will now each collect $200.

The lady of the house is about to discover that Henry's Fork is not a new tableware pattern, and that

6, 8, and 10 do not necessarily refer to dress sizes. The phrase "for better or worse" has taken on a new meaning.

Someone once wrote words to the effect "for much of the summer a great many people will be ill-housed, ill-fed, and ill-clothed..." I don't know for sure, but the author might have been referring to a fishing vacation. How can a man delude himself into believing that his loved ones would enjoy watching him (or maybe not watching him) match wits with fish? Why the people involved go along with this delusion is most often a mystery as well. Yet I see them everywhere— bug-ridden, half-frozen, or sunburned; living examples of the anesthetic effects of boredom.

(It is true, I'm pleased to report, that more and more women are taking up fly fishing. I'm positive this is because a lot of women have watched the head of the household for a while and become convinced that they can do it at least as well, probably better.)

By now our man David has discovered that there are more new horizons than simply the accumulation of gear. His fellow anglers have been name-dropping. They are into big numbers and faraway places, and David has gotten the impression that some of the stories might contain a grain of truth. He has also discovered that the earth tilts and rotates around the sun and that while he is shoveling snow in Illinois, some of his peers are casting to bonefish in Mexico or "legendary" browns in New Zealand. David is not slow to react. Travel brochures screaming GIANT...WORLD RECORD...UNSPOILED are scattered through his house. The pictures show strong men straining to heft rainbow trout or dwarfed by tarpon. David sees exotic labels on his rod case, and hears himself talking about kilos and meters. He is delighted that the catalogs have 800 numbers and 24-hour-a-day order takers.

Our fly man can now take a reel apart and clean it, and he can tie several knots that will actually stay tied. He has tested all this and worked on his fighting technique by looping fifty-pound mono to the collar of his Labrador retriever, which has come to love playing the role of a tarpon. Her name is *Salmo Salar*, but she answers to "Salty."

In time the rest of the family becomes hooked on fly fishing. They don't really have a choice. Now, of an evening, the family gathers to watch videos on long-distance casting, steelhead on the Babine, sailfish off Costa Rica, advanced dry-fly methods, and the like. Sometimes David reads aloud from Lyons or Wulff or Haig-Brown while his wife ties up leaders and the children reorganize his fly boxes. Like so many other fishermen, David spends his mental time mostly in another world, and finds it to be a far better place than the real one he lives in.

A family could do worse. Recently, I asked David's wife what she liked most about her family's fishing.

"It's just wonderful," she said. "Now everybody's so easy to buy presents for!"

21

GENE'S
GEMS

Ever since I first read the witty and timeless essays that appear in Ben Franklin's *Poor Richard's Almanac*, I have been collecting special little phrases to live by. These homilies seem to rise and fall on some strange tide, and lately, the tide seems to be higher than usual. So I've come up with a few sayings of my own. I claim no originality for these gems, nor am I suggesting that they will always hold true. But I have recorded them faithfully and offer herewith a small selection:

- Never criticize another man's dog—even if he asks you.
- Smart dog-owners never say never, and they never say always. But they always give their dogs the benefit of the doubt.
- Few things make me feel better than petting a dog. Worry seems to flow out through my fingertips.

- Never brag about your shooting ability, especially before you start shooting.
- Why do so many of us think that good equipment is a substitute for practice?
- The best shooting instructor is a case of shells.
- Check the trigger pull on your guns at least once a year. Like clothes, a trap gun can change its own measurements.
- Always carry a screwdriver that fits your gun.
- Everybody misses easy shots.
- There are no easy shots.
- Before you shoot at something a long way off, think about how long it will take you to get there.
- There is no such thing as being too safe with a firearm—any firearm.
- Don't hunt with people who make you nervous.
- Whenever you find something you really like, buy two, or three, before they change it or stop making it.
- The more remote a gas station is, the earlier it closes. It will never be open on Sundays.
- If you ask anyone—even a friend—for directions, you'll still get lost at least 50 percent of the time, maybe more.
- If you've never been lost, you've never been far from home.
- Local knowledge and real knowledge aren't always the same.

- Always ask your guide to repeat the directions about where you'll meet later. Twice.
- Never underestimate your guide. Chances are he knows more about his business than you do about yours.
- Always tell a guide you're five years older than you really are.
- Good fly casters always get the best guides.
- When you fall in a river, you're no longer a fisherman; you're a swimmer.
- Falling in is one of the most exciting things that ever happens to a fisherman. It brings out the little boy in him.
- No one in any camp ever has extra bootlaces.
- When you break the hook on a fly, you'll get a hit on the next cast.
- Any knot you tie in a hurry comes untied the same way.
- The worst waste of money is a cheap pair of binoculars.
- Using a fly rod guarantees windy fishing conditions.
- Always carry a spare ignition key. Better, carry two, in different places.
- When that once-in-a-lifetime trip opportunity comes up, grab it, even if you think you can't afford it.
- The longer the trip, the more stuff you will take that you don't need.

- If only trips were as much fun as planning them.
- Trips that include women are more fun than those that don't. The same is not true of children.
- Give your kids a tree book and a bird book to take on your trip. Then you can ask them what you don't know.
- The best thing to bring to a new place is an open mind.
- What counts on a trip is not how good you are, but how much fun you are.
- Beautiful guns don't necessarily shoot better than plain ones, but they always seem to.
- A woman who tells her husband to "have a good time" is always beautiful.
- Always pay your own share—and a little more.
- Lying down and looking up at the clouds makes you feel younger.
- Everyone else is just as afraid of lightning as you are.
- Don't brag about your equipment or skills. One is obvious, and the other will soon be.
- No matter how good you are, someone is always better.
- Some people *are* luckier than others.
- A man with a really good gun probably knows how to shoot it.
- I never made an enemy by praising someone's shooting—or his dog.

22

MORE THAN
A CRAFT

Not so many years ago in America, the shotgun pretty well symbolized a national attitude. If the mainspring on your Parker broke or the firing pin snapped on your L. C. Smith, chances were good that the village blacksmith could do some creative tinkering, making a new part, and get you back into the bird field or the duck marsh in short order.

As American shotgun and rifle design evolved over the years, a lot of those tinkerers taught themselves the craft of gunsmithing. Today, scattered across the country, there are highly skilled gunsmiths whose establishments serve as meeting places for boys of all ages who come to watch the master at work and to talk about the important things in life—like guns and hunting and bird dogs and deer stands.

It's easy for me to find an excuse to visit George, since there is usually something rattling around or gone cranky in one or more of my guns. I like to hang over the bench and watch as the magician's fingers extract springs and screws and hooks and other parts as mysterious to me as spleens and kidneys. When George finishes rustling around inside my bird gun, it shoots at least as well as when it was new, and sometimes better.

Any time is a good time to hang around a gunsmith's shop, but the atmosphere is at fever pitch the week before hunting season opens. All of us who have been promising not to wait until the last minute find ourselves pulling into the crowded driveway and walking into a happy bedlam where the aromas of machine oil, old hunting clothes, and boot dubbing blend in perfectly. The NO SMOKING sign is obscured by pipe tobacco. George is trying to answer questions from the floor—the same questions he answered last year the week before hunting season. The man with the loose recoil pad is handed a screwdriver and a little boy holding his father's hand gets some homemade candy. George knows that his holding most of the guns and peering down the barrels will generally "fix" them. He somehow knows instinctively which guns really need work and which ones just rattle a little, and probably always did and always will.

The gathering of the clan is part of the annual ritual; before we can go on to opening day, we must pass through George's place to wring out one more hour or so of tingling anticipation. I usually end up buying a pair of gloves or a box of shells that I don't need, and pretending to sharpen my knife on the public whetstone, so I can listen to the other loafers. Maybe I can pick up some information about early woodcock flights or a hint about a new grouse cover. I hope at least someone will ask my opinion about duck loads or get me into a deep discussion about improved-cylinder bores or 28-gauge bird guns.

George has discovered a young boy who needs a stock cut down to fit him and I know from past experience that this will take priority. The measurements are done with scientific precision, although I know that George can tell at a glance what they ought to be, down to the last millimeter. George produces a new shell vest and tells the boy to put it on so "proper measurements" can be taken. The boy is not used to many new clothes; George has noted that and explains, as he has done before, that "this old vest is just taking up room and you'd be doing me a favor to keep it on; I've been hoping someone your size would show up so I could get it out of my way..." or some such similar yarn that forbids any argument. Now and then I have seen George "trade" a vest for the promise of a rabbit or a pair of squirrels.

I slept in my first hunting vest, bothered only by the fact that I didn't have enough shells to fill up all the elastic loops. It's good to know that George is still part small boy and part gentleman who understands such things.

23

WING
TIPS

Unless your memory is a lot better than mine, you probably don't recall that I've written about dove shooting from time to time. Naturally, the ammunition companies have asked me to cease and desist because they worry that my expertise will ultimately make the readers better shooters and thus depress the shotshell market. But as always, I will fearlessly continue to do my duty as I see it.

When I'm shooting a 12 at doves, I like a modi-fied choke, and on very windy days I'll go to full. Under perfect conditions an improved-cylinder will do but I so rarely experience ideal conditions that I'm not sure exactly what they are.

I also like No. 7½ shot and wouldn't weep if all I had were No. 6s. Most guns pattern these sizes quite well and I like the little extra energy they pro-vide. No. 8s and 9s don't seem to put birds down quite as well. Argue with me all you want, bearing in mind that I don't hear very well on this subject. A one-ounce load will do very well and the reduction in recoil is a blessing for those of us who occasionally miss just to see if it's possible.

One of the most overlooked causes of missing, other than not really staying down on the stock, is a too heavy trigger pull. By too heavy I mean over 3½ pounds. A heavy or sticky trigger will cause you to pull the barrel down and over, turning a perfectly led bird into a clean miss. If you do nothing else with your gun before bird season, at least have the pull checked.

I still like the "come from behind and swing through" method on doves, and I'll add two more tips to that. The first is to shoot *slightly* under a dove, since it will dive more often than zoom up; the second is to take a fraction longer to *really look* at the bird so it is in clear focus before you shoot. I mean *clear*—not fuzzy or indistinct. Not taking this extra effort is one of the major causes of missing anything, clay targets included. Trust me on this.

And here's another tip. Don't take a death grip on the fore-end! Place your index finger along the side of the fore-end—or extend it as if you were using it to point at the bird—and let the gun rest gently in your extended palm. Trust me on this, too, even though it might feel strange at first.

Of all the major faults that result in missing, trying to be too careful is near the top. Shotguns are not aimed, they're pointed. A shotgun is not an artillery piece. It should be mounted, swung, and fired in a minimal amount of time. In general, the quicker you shoot after the butt touches your shoulder, the better.

Your first impression of the proper lead is almost always the right one. Trust that, too.

We all have our own ideas about the hardest dove shot. If you're right-handed and are missing too many right-to-left crossing shots, you might be a bit left-eye dominant. Try closing the left eye a little as you swing through. If you see a lot of the barrel side with both eyes open and little or none with the left eye closed, you definitely should try using just the right eye at the last second.

The common cause of missing left-to-right crossing doves is taking your cheek off the stock and losing the proper alignment of your eye and the barrel. Stay down firmly and see what good things can happen.

The high incomer offers several fine ways to miss. Commonly you shoot off to one side of the dove because you want to see it very clearly, and when the bird is taken properly, it's a bit obscured by the gun barrel. Try starting slightly behind the bird and shoot just as the barrel comes past the head. Be careful of tracking too long here, as you want to shoot when the bird is a bit out front, not directly overhead.

If there's one major fault most of us dove shooters have (I know it's mine), it's being careless with gun mounting. I like to take a few minutes several times a day to practice this, making sure the butt is in the shoulder pocket, the head is firmly on the stock, and the fore-end is cradled, not squeezed. If your head is off the stock as little as an inch, it can change the height of the pattern as much as three feet at thirty-five yards.

I realize that much of what I've put down here is rudimentary, but shooting decently—which is taking one dove for three shells—isn't all that hard, most of the time. What happens to the other two shells is what keeps us coming back; the sweet mystery of wingshooting. I remember a day last season when I took six straight doves, and then missed the next six on identical chances. I went from believing I might have been born a dove shooter to wondering if I'd live long enough to get the limit.

Incidentally, I was once shooting with a man who only took the high incoming shots and almost never missed. I was impressed because those shots can make me look foolish, to put it kindly. I later found out that he wouldn't take any other shot because he couldn't hit any other angle and decided he'd specialize. I kind of like that idea and just as soon as I can find an angle I'm good at, I might do exactly the same thing.

An old-timer once told me that a dove knows when you're pointing at it and can dodge the shot, more often than not. I used to laugh at that, but now that I'm getting old, I'm not so sure that he wasn't right.

24

MODEST
ADMISSIONS

I hesitate to elaborate further on my dove shooting secrets. So many folks have followed my advice like gospel that the ammunition companies are hurting and a couple of states are altering season dates and restricting the limits.

Gun sales are probably off too. In fact, the only real bright spot is that more and more dove shooters are spending more and more time with their families, taking the wife and children to cultural centers and such, instead of spending so much time in the field with their shooting buddies. I feel proud to have played a small part in helping restructure their family lives. No, I don't need public thanks; just knowing what good I've done is more than enough reward.

It was hard to believe at first, but I'm now used to requests about how to sort of "fringe" doves, since so many of my readers were centering them with an excess of 7½'s. All you have to do is remember that a dove will only move about sixteen inches a second and adjust accordingly. Simple when you think of it; you only need to know whether your shotload is one that has a velocity of 1200 feet per second, or one of those that's slightly faster, say about 1400 fps.

There's something else that seems to work *against* everyone, although I don't know why—bragging about your wingshooting ability. In case you want to challenge this fact of life, it's important to remember that the *size* of the brag is not a factor; even if you make only a modest (non-Texan) admission that you are fairly handy with a 20-bore, you are cursed. And the more people who hear your brag or who are watching you shoot, the worse it is.

One of my favorite tricks to increase the ratio of shells to bird is to fire the first shot two or three feet behind the bird, which makes it dive, thereby turning a routine crossing shot into one that approaches the impossible. No one, not a Fred Kimble, a Rudy Etchen, or a Barry Allison can do much with a diving target. I also like to refuse to pick out one bird in a flock, and instead just throw shot at the whole bunch. If you score at all doing this, be sure and buy a lottery ticket that very evening.

One reader tells me that after taking eight or ten doves with as many shells, he likes to prolong the day by placing himself where he can see the birds coming from a distance. He says this strategy teases him into mounting his gun early and then tracking the flight and measuring the *exact* lead—about three feet, 9¼ inches for a thirty-five-yard, 90-degree crossing bird. The best he's done is eleven zeros in a row. He claims

he'd have improved on that, but someone borrowed his last few shells.

For those of you who would like to go through a whole box of shells when the limit is only twelve or fifteen birds, and no matter how hard you try doves still seem to hit the ground, I offer you the Adams Gambit. Almost any gun will do but a cheap double is much preferred. The stock has to be at least two inches too short, the trigger pull set at no less than six pounds, and the butt plate should be either steel or bare wood. The gauge must be 12 and the loads should be at least 3¼ drams. The first three or four shots ought to give you a decent headache and hopefully a slightly puffy nose. Not many of us are man enough to handle this, but here is sportsmanship at its best. When you get hurt more than the dove, I salute you, unless you're from Texas, of course.

I missed a dove last year (yes, I have witnesses) that left me puzzled. It was a run-of-the-mill down-wind left-to-right crossing shot. The breeze couldn't have been gusting over thirty mph and I doubt if the bird was an inch more than forty-five yards away. Routine, you say, and I agree, but although I drew feathers, the bird never faltered. There was a lot of discussion about it right after evening prayers, so I got the gun down from the rack and looked it over very carefully. I checked the choke markings and they were IC, as I'd thought, which was why I'd led the bird forty-one inches. Then it dawned on me. I turned to the owner of the gun and asked if he'd had any work done on the choke. He told me he'd had the barrel swagged down to modified, which meant, of course, that I should have been holding a little tighter—about thirty-eight inches. Of such small details are legends made and lost.

If you're one of the few who is still worried about a limit on about as many shells, let me quote to you from a book on dove hunting: "It's not difficult...

swinging the barrel, focusing the eyes on the bird flying at fifty-five feet per second with a shot string traveling at 1200 feet per second...your subconscious computer can handle the problem easily..."

You can't argue the simplicity of that, can you? Which returns us to our problem of preventing boredom by being able to hear the gun go off without this being followed by a soft thud of bird striking the ground. You can practice this on a skeet field, as I often do. Right now I know I can consistently shoot behind high three and low six, common angles in the dove field. I could learn to miss others I suppose, but I don't feel the need.

One of the great pleasures I get now is overhearing snippets of conversation like, "You're not going to believe it but Hill missed two doves today! Saw it with my own eyes. Probably up all night working...does it all the time..." Just as well they don't know how hard it's been for me to stifle my lightning reflexes and thwart my incredible hand/eye coordination, and concentrate on shooting where they were rather than where they're going to be. It's like trying to unlearn swimming or riding a bicycle.

In olden days it was considered a great mark of honor to have "He hath slain the lion" engraved as an epitaph. It might be written on my stone, "He hath missed the dove." A man does what he can...keeping up with the changing times.

25

PATINA, INC.

While I was throwing some stuff together for a fishing trip recently, my old fly vest literally fell apart. This was a disaster; it's one thing for a beginner to show up in a new vest, but it's unthinkable for an old salt to do so.

As I pondered the vanity of the average outdoorsman, however, it suddenly hit me, in one of those rare insights, that perhaps I could turn that vanity into a public service and substantially raise my standard of living. I just hope the outdoor world is ready for this kind of quantum-leap thinking.

For years the kids have been buying "weathered" stuff. If it works for them, why not for a long-suffering fellow like me? I know that I can arrange, for a reasonable fee, to have virtually any outdoor garment broken in perfectly, to give it that nice patina of usage—and more.

Now, consider your new duck gun. You know that a duck gun ought never to look new. Think of your credibility as the old swamper, the guy who has faced a thousand dawns and sunsets. Well, relax. My firm can use it for you. Consider our A-Grade special, which only takes a couple of weeks. Our metal specialists will remove the perfect amount of bluing and carefully add a few battle scars. The sworn letter of authentication you receive will list all the pertinent facts. It might read as follows:

"The long vertical scratch on the left side of the stock came from a nail in the famous Pintail Blind at the Beaver Dam Club in Tennessee. The slight crack in the fore-end was the result of Brad Dysinger (high overall at last year's Grand American) swinging on a hard left angle and hitting a metal brace in the blind. The photograph shows Brad holding your fine gun and his limit..."

We can, of course, customize your letter any way you would like, although we urge you to use discretion in creating your story.

Consider the effect you'll have on friends and acquaintances when you display your eight-weight rod and casually point out that the off-colored wrapping on the second guide from the tip-top was done by _____ (here we allow you to choose from a list of famous names in our employ), on _____ (here you choose from a list of storied rivers, domestic or international). Your letter might read like this:

"Dear Mike: Many thanks for letting me use your rod on the (*river name here*). Sorry about the little mishap with the guide; it happened at the net and was unavoidable. You know all too well how that goes, especially with (*fish species here*) in the record class. Your angling friend, _____. P.S. I've sent off under separate cover a copy of my new book on Argentina and I think you'll find that chapter four brings back warm memories."

The possibilities are endless. Can't you see yourself casually pointing out a small patch on your shooting jacket sleeve and remarking in your understated way, "Strand of barbed wire on the Duke's place in Scotland." Or, "I never dreamed that just a few days of driven pheasant in Yorkshire could do this to the fore-end; it's practically scorched!" Perhaps, "I've thought about getting this little ding repaired—here at the toe of the stock—but then it isn't every day one's gun gets carried around in a mule wagon in Georgia—whenever I notice it, I'm reminded of twenty coveys plus."

Admittedly, those are A Grades. But for a little less we can arrange for a Jim Bashline salmon fly to be artfully, obviously, and permanently embedded in your sweater—"Bashline did that on the St. Jean"—or a Jimmy Albright tarpon fly in the sleeve of your slicker— "You know how the wind can come up off Islamorada." A couple of very nice touches, if you ask me.

I'm still working on a list of options and other pertinent details, but one I know will be popular is my bird shooting safari in Tanzania. I expect I can run through six or eight guns, maybe more, in a few days. It won't be cheap and it has to be first come, first served. At the other end of the scale I expect to be able to arrange for Dave Petzal to sharpen your knife; it will, of course, come back with a brief note and an appropriate dateline, with Colorado or Montana at the low end, and Zambia or the like for a few bob extra.

I doubt if we'll be able to accept anything much smaller than a fly box or larger than a matched pair of double guns, but these things remain to be seen. We probably won't be able to accept personal items such as underwear, but a hunting coat used as an emergency saddle blanket in British Columbia would be everyday stuff, and I can see a dozen pairs of binoculars getting a little weathered in a hunting car in Botswana. You dream it up—I'll try to do it!

It may be a little down the road, but I can see making arrangments with the major catalog houses to have your stuff shipped directly to us. If domestic difficulties loom and there is a need to cover up the purchase of a fine piece of sporting equipment, we can arrange for a variety of covering letters. For example:

"Dear _____: You have been randomly selected to use *(item goes here)* and give us your candid opinion. We insist that you keep _____ as a token of our appreciation."

"Dear _____: A friend, who wishes to remain unnamed, has asked us to ship you this _____ as a small gesture of his respect."

Or, simply, "Dear _____: Please hold this for me for a while as my wife is not quite as understanding as yours. Please *(shoot it/fish it/etc.)* as you wish; treat it as if it were yours."

Well, you get the idea. Just the bare bones so far, but it's easy to see that we're working with something as big as all outdoors!

If you've always wanted that little touch, that something special to make your sporting image a mirror of your real self, just remember our motto: "To Hill With It!"

26

SOUNDS

I was fooling around with the house dog the other day, trying to see if I could shut the icebox door so quietly that she couldn't hear it from her sofa in the other room. I don't know how she could have heard it. Maybe she's just tuned to that sound—and why not? She doesn't have all that much else to do.

Anyway, I got thinking about *unwelcome* sounds I've heard over the years. I still remember the hollow *click* of a firing pin falling on an empty chamber during a heavy money shoot-off in a pigeon match. Another sound, not uncommon with me, is the little crack you hear when you snap off the only fly that raised a fish all day. I have also heard the sickening sound of a fine cane rod snapping at the tip after some overly frenetic power casting.

I suppose everybody knows the curious, dreaded clatter that tells you the outboard is absolutely, positively not going to start. The grinding crunch of a rock along a canoe bottom is another dreaded sound. And how can you ever forget the machine-gun notes of a bird dog's bell after she has jumped a deer and decided to run it down or die trying.

Dogs have a lot of built-in sounds waiting for the perfect moment to be aired. How about the faithful retriever who sleeps calmly but protectively by your bedside and waits until 3 A.M. to get sick to her stomach? Or the throaty low rumble that harks back to the cave days and means *something* is out there? Why dogs never do this during daylight hours is beyond me, but so are a lot of other things.

Sounds do not have to be all that loud to get your attention and remind you that some days are going to be more interesting than others. A simple calamity is the *snap* of your already twice-knotted boot lace breaking; no one ever seems to have a spare. Any sound signifying part of a horse's saddlery breaking carries a note of special horror for me; I fully expect to be involved with a runaway, without the brakes working.

Sitting down on your only pair of glasses isn't very noisy, but I'll bet you recognize the sound the second it happens. Clothing gives up so commonly at the wrong places and times that it really isn't worth mentioning. But there is the dreaded silence of the stuck zipper on your sleeping bag and guess what the temperature is outside? This is best combined with the funny click of the flashlight that isn't going to flash or the faint deathly breath of the gas lantern when there's no fuel. After dark, of course, always brings out the bizarre aspect of otherwise common sounds. The beginning of my gray hair might well have started one night when a beaver slapped his tail in the pond that (a) I couldn't see and (b) I didn't know was there. Until that moment, I didn't know a beaver could make a noise that could elevate a grown man three feet in the air.

Creaking trees, squirrels on tin roofs, and the tinkle of running water coming from a place where there shouldn't be running water are all designed to intently focus your mind for a mysterious moment or two.

On a recent hunting trip, I heard a strange midnight sound emanating from a tentside woodpile. It took a tremendous amount of courage to investigate and discover a porcupine having a late snack inside the woodpile. It wasn't quite what my imagination was working on, but I was more than pleased, and it only took me two hours or so to get back to sleep.

I also listen carefully now for sounds that I missed the first time around: the muted fall of water over a four-foot dam that I almost, but not quite, cleared in a canoe; or the low bellow of a Jersey bull from an unseen corner of a meadow where I was rabbit hunting.

I should have prefaced all this by mentioning that I have always been a little hard of hearing—it runs in the family—so messages of some importance are often missed, or worse, misinterpreted. "I wouldn't wade there if I were you," is one where I've missed the critical phrase. Another that looms large in my memory is my brother mumbling something about a sticky throttle on his motorcycle. Why certain people remember these things years later, with whoops of laughter, is beyond me. I suppose it's indicative of the deep streak of cruelty that mankind exhibits from time to time.

The human voice can be used quite effectively to project a degree of dread or pain. What sound is more obvious than the merriment of your partner reminding you, as he lands his sixth fish, that you haven't caught any? What about the "wolf in sheep's clothing" voice of the guy who barely beat you in a shoot-off saying it was just his lucky day? Then there's the midnight tone in a woman's voice as she reminds you that you swore you'd be back by 6 P.M. at the latest. And the thin sound of your own thin voice reminding you that this is where you'd swear you left the truck...

There are sounds, and sounds. The warden's voice, triumphant, telling you that you forgot to sign the state bird stamp...the smug voice saying "three kings" as you lay down three jacks...the vet, stumbling over his words as he tries to explain what happened with

Old Pete...the hardware store clerk telling you, "I sold my last box of 20s to the guy that just walked out the door"...the flat, innocent tone of voice when a guide says, "You've got to get more out in front of these wild birds"...or someone else says, "That dog never bit anybody before!"...or "Does this look like the right road to you?"

If I had to list one all-time sound I could live forever without, but probably won't, it could be the crack of nearby lightning when I'm in the middle of big water in a small metal boat. Or, it could be the breaking of glass and the expletive deleted when someone drops the only bottle of the good stuff the first night in camp. I don't even want to *think* about the sound of my editor's voice on the telephone asking: "You don't, by any chance, have another copy of your upcoming column, do you? We never received the original..."

27

Labels, Signs, and Portents

When I was shooting live pigeons with some regularity, I favored a particular brand of shotgun shell that had a white pigeon on it. Noticing that my supply of 7½'s was running low, I called up a pal who worked for the company and said I wanted to buy a case of such shells. He said their xyz load was exactly the same but sold for a little less.

"Does it have the little white pigeon on it?" I asked.

"No," he said, "but it's the same shell. You don't want to spend more if you don't need to, right?"

"Wrong. If it doesn't have the pigeon, it's not a real pigeon load."

When you're talking intellect vs. superstition, superstition wins every time. So, needless to say, my pigeon gun had not one, but three pigeons on it. Did they actually help? Quite possibly. Who knows how bad I'd have been without them.

My basic woodcock gun, a 28-gauge Parker Reproduction, also has not one but three woodcock engraved on it. Nothing inconsistent about me! My tarpon fly reels have TARPON written on them, and I would be tempted to part with a little of the egg money if I could get my hands on a new "CAST LONGER AND EASIER" fly rod.

My favorite old duck gun was so stamped— DUCK GUN. It gave me no end of confidence, as do the words THE ALASKAN on my .338 magnum, in case I ever decide to have at it with a Kodiak bear or a moose with a six-foot set of antlers.

Be honest now, don't you feel better—more correct, more confident—knowing that your whitetail rifle barrel has the word DEERSLAYER, or some such, on it? You'd be foolish not to admit you'd have more faith in such a gun. Even such a simple instrument as a magnetic compass, which by its very nature points to N, wouldn't be acceptable to you without that unnecessary N on it. You wouldn't touch it. Right?

Today the hot outdoor sport is sporting clays. My sporting gun, in almost all respects identical to my skeet gun, was added to my modest armory on the basis of these words of promise—SPORTING CLAYS— engraved on the receiver. Needless to say, I would never use the skeet gun to shoot sporting or vice versa.

I find it very comforting to be able to look over the shelf and find a box of 20s boldly labeled DOVE AND QUAIL. Who among us would ever consider just another box of plain old light 8s when you're gearing up for doves or quail? I once owned a gun, a rather sleek 16-gauge side-by-side, that had a quail on the side plates. But I never shot it particularly well and now I believe that the quail was a maker's error and that the gun should have been engraved with a pheasant. Or a zero.

As deeply hooked as I am by labels, signs, and portents, I have to admit that many manufacturers have played pretty hard with our innocent faith. Even I don't feel any more thoroughly costumed in a duck hunting

shirt with a neon mallard stitched on the pocket, or a pair of suspenders stenciled with trout flies. Clothes aren't really equipment anyway, with the exception of neckties. A tie sporting Labradors or a sprinkling of Royal Wulffs or grouse feathers can lead you into conversations with like-minded people on occasions when showing up in your fishing vest or brush pants would put you at instant odds with the Queen Bee.

If all this seems frivolous and childish, think again. Many of man's oldest weapons were marked in the same way. Indian quivers often were decorated with the likenesses of buffalo, bears, deer, or elk. A brave's knife was wrapped in a carefully chosen animal skin, and axes and tomahawks were etched with symbols of the hunt. I may not be even a shadow of the Indian hunter, but at least the same traditions are still honored for the same reasons. Wishing ourselves luck never hurt.

In the days of sail, the cannon were often named; the same was true for artillery and other weapons. In later wars, bombers and fighters were named and decorated with battle marks, as were submarines and other vessels. Before that, pistols were notched by successful gunfighters and it was the rare frontier rifle that didn't display some mark or sign of the owner's trust and affection. As often as not in those days, a man's rifle was the only friend he felt he could count on.

I'm pretty sure that my sheer delight in sporting marks—a tasteful little grouse engraved on the trigger guard of a 20-bore, a colorful salmon fly painted on a favorite rod, a skinning knife with a handle made from the horns of a deer I shot—reveals more than just my artistic side. I think it also has something to do with how we have "softened" our lethal tools over the millennia.

Or maybe it goes deeper than that—back to our ancient beginnings when the relationship between the hunter and the hunted was woven more tightly with fear and need; when the hunter and the hunted were often changing places; when sport was the least of it.

28

SIMPLE MOVES

It's hard not to take issue with the masters who tell us, while casting ninety feet of fly line with their thumbs and forefingers, "This isn't hard when you make these simple moves..." Then they show us a pig-tailed Brownie hauling the whole fly line.

It has not been easy to admit that a ten-year-old girl with an arm like a knitting needle can do this. Maybe she can also run 100 straight with the 20-gauge, but I refuse to dwell on that. What I *am* dwelling on is that *I* can't throw the whole fly line, at least not well, or often.

I never wanted to run a four-minute mile or be a dazzling light-heavy, but I do believe that to think of yourself as a good fly fisherman, you ought to be able to throw the whole line at will. I think it improves your normal casting technique and solves a lot of windy day problems. And last but not least, you can sure annoy most of your fishing pals who can't do it...

Yes, I *have* taken lessons and they do help. But the minute the instructor leaves, my less-than-perfect timing returns with a vengeance; wind knots the size of sour grapes appear as if by magic in the leader, and rod manufacturers who thought they'd seen everything have been known to weep. I've spent my egg money for tapes and books, but they merely deepen the frustration. I have nightmares of nurslings snatched from their mothers' laps roll-casting eighty feet and laying out long curve casts with rake handles.

Left alone, my consistent best effort is a little better than seventy feet; give me the nod and say seventy-five, but the last fifteen feet just don't shoot. Where is that magical little touch that sends the backing humming through the guides? Where is the payoff for honesty and hard work they promised me in Sunday school?

And success is as mysterious as failure. The one cast that does come alive and brings the backing knot out of hiding happens often as not when you least want it, sending the Royal Wulff deep into the willows or lining the one big feeding trout. But there *is* that one brief moment of satisfaction...

I had a whole morning just like that, fishing for Atlantic salmon on the George River in Quebec. A photographer was filming me and it was one of those very rare days when the line was long and straight and the loops tight, and I looked like I knew what I was doing. No doubt I had a favorable wind. The downside was that although we knew there were fresh fish in our stretch of river, I wasn't catching any. So I went off to another pool and a beginning angler whose best cast couldn't have reached forty feet took my place and proceeded to take six nice salmon running fifteen to twenty pounds. If I'd known those fish were lying so close, would I have been content to stand there and throw only half the line I was capable of throwing—in front of a camera? Sure, but not every time.

One of my fishing pals, knowing my love for eight-, nine-, and ten-weight rods has, with some disdain, called me a "jock strap fisherman." I admit to it. I lack the patience and delicacy to toss size 18 and 20 flies to soft, sipping rises. I'm happiest heaving big Zonkers, Matukas, and other stuff the size of a house wren as far across the river as I can. When I was a small boy I believed that the farther away the fish were the bigger they had to be. I guess I still think so.

I'm not at all sure that my seventy-five-foot limit isn't genetic, like my inability to leap no higher than a foot and a half in the air. But I have practiced. I have also sought the answer in a mad frenzy of rod buying— the time-honored refuge of the inept. I have had rods from virtually every major, and a few minor, makers in the U.S. and several from England and France. I've ended up with a few favorites, rods I actually caught fish with. The other day I dug out one of these, an old Orvis boron/graphite for a nine-weight line, to try something I saw on a new casting video. I was pleasingly surprised at how good this outfit felt in the hand, and after a few false casts to get the kinks out of the line, I tried my best to come up to the level of the schoolgirls shown on the casting film. The second or third cast sent the whole fly line out past the rod tip! It was almost as effortless as promised, and I felt I could share a pool with any eighth-grader and not feel foolish.

But then I suddenly remembered last using this rod and reel setup on a big river in Canada where the guides keep you fishing one beat until you have cast the whole fly line or close to it before they moved the canoe to the next drop. If you couldn't hack the casting, the guides would grumble and make disparaging remarks.

After one particularly frustrating afternoon, I asked myself why I should be one of the sheep. Where is it written you have to listen to grumbling remarks or that a fly line has to be ninety feet long? So I cut fifteen feet or so off the back of my line. I'm happy to report that the guides were thrilled with my improved distance and none the wiser.

You'll be happy to know that this tactic also works with tarpon and bonefish guides. The moral here is pretty straightforward: If you can't reach what you're grasping for, find a way to stand a little closer.

29

GIANT
THOUGHTS

I sit in a small boat in the great Pacific, my stare fixed on the wake of the baits, watching for the probing bill or the tip of the dorsal.

I close my eyes for a moment's rest and the blue marlin that hangs from chains in the dining room at the hotel in Cabo San Lucas comes into focus. Majestic and arrogant even in painted plaster, with cold unblinking eyes, it seems poised to shear the water at sixty miles an hour. I can picture that great fish idling under the baits thinking marlin thoughts; instinct weighing energy and effort against food and survival. I make a wish, half in hope, half in fear, wondering what it's like to lean against a fish five times your size that will resist until the end.

If the contest was a simple tug-of-war, a rope that tied the two of us together, I would not be there. Without the mechanical advantages of the boat, the rod, the pail-sized reel, I would be thinking much smaller thoughts. My dining room marlin could tow me fast enough to peel my skin. It could tear my arms from their sockets, explode my lungs in the deep, or pierce

my body with its bill without any more malice than I would grant to a breakfast sausage.

But I wish this imaginary fish no harm. I only want to know what it can teach me about power and courage. And to see it hanging improbably against the sky would be the ultimate—like pulling a 1,000-pound rabbit out of a 100-fathom hat.

In a way the small brook, the pond, the river, and the sea are all the same to the fisherman. They are places for the imagination to play—a bass by every stump, a trout behind every stone, a marlin in the trough of every wave. We tie hope to our line and send it out into the mystery water. Then we wait, boy and man alike, for the answer to the same question.

The captain heels the boat to follow a flight of frigate birds. Suddenly where there was nothing I see 100 porpoises cutting through a school of tuna. The yellowfins are in the air and I can feel their terror. Two small striped marlin are in the air with them, leaping and twisting. Chunks of tuna drift on the surface and swooping birds spoon them with their bills. As suddenly as it started, it's done. Two or three minutes have passed on the inexorable clock. Everyone on the boat feels a little older. Everyone has a cold beer.

The ocean is a little different now. I see it as a busy place. Tuna hurrying about their business, porpoises lolling around, the marlin solitary and menacing, running their deep intercepts on schools of squid, always watching, remorselessly driven by a primal nerve that carries a single message from brain to gut. The frigate birds rest their slender wings on the warm thermals, waiting for scraps.

Time to daydream again. I know there is no half-ton blue marlin here, even though I can *feel* one. No, I don't *know*. That's the odd part of fishing most of the time—not knowing anything a lot of the time. You think it could be here, right under your bait, and you remember the sea stories, and all the fishing tales of wonder and surprise.

Here, at least, fishing is indeed the art of the possible. I see the giant blue off the coast of Australia, passing Hawaii, turning off the coast of California, looking for me near the Sea of Cortez. Long-liners have taken some blues that weighed 2,000 pounds. Twice as big as my dining room vision. Bigger than I can fit into a dream, larger than imagination, beyond ken. Unreal.

I hadn't planned to run a bait for a big blue. I was here to try to catch a small striped marlin on a fly rod, and for some reason—the curse of fishing probably—that wasn't working out and I turned my mind the other way. In general, I don't like trolling or big boat tackle, and I'm not into "record book" fishing. But here I sit involved in two out of the three. For no good or sane reason, I want to see something huge. The ten-year-old inside me is having a good time while the rest of me looks on somewhat puzzled. I guess I'm not fishing as much as I'm being curious.

The boat makes a lazy-eight between two shore points, time and again. The captain has a notion about this spot and guards it from other boats. It's almost like sitting on a deer trail thinking, *This is the way he has to come*. I wonder what makes this spot special and ask the captain in English. The answer, in Spanish, is the same one the guides always give, even if you don't understand the exact words: "It's a good place." That doesn't answer my question, but fishing's often just a matter of faith.

Late in the afternoon, the captain tells me the day is over. Time to leave. I wonder, as always, what if we made one more pass? Was the fish coming up to the bait just as we turned to head back? What if...

In the dining room the waiter asks if I have seen a fish this big—*ever*—as he looks at the giant blue on chains. I want to say *always*, but I just smile and shake my head no. I think he's glad I said that, and I understand. Some things are best only wished for, better left out there, to be fished for rather than caught.

"*Mañana,*" he says with a smile. I echo the thought. Tomorrow is always the very best day for fishing.

30

DREAMS
OF GLORY

Somewhere along the line I lost my little trout reel, the one I like for my four-weight rod. So I started digging through my catalogs to find a decent but not too expensive replacement. The lost reel was an old Hardy that now costs about ten times what I paid for it. The new reel I settled on isn't nearly as elegant as the Hardy, and I really hoped to find something sleeker... Actually I was a bit crushed, since I have a large weak spot for fly reels and can recite the names and the specs of the great ones with the ease of a monk tolling the saints.

You know how one thing leads to another in the idle mind, so I got to wondering just how much you could spend on a fly reel. Let's say one right "off the shelf." Admittedly, it's one off the high shelf, but that's an interesting place to look now and then.

If you were paid what you're worth and shared my lack of self-restraint, you could rather easily find an Abel marlin reel for less than $2,000. For about $1,500, if you're lucky enough to locate one, you can have a Bogdan salmon reel, truly a work of high art. But forget ordering from Stan Bogdan; he's back-ordered to the millennium or longer. So let's restrict ourselves to relatively current and available stuff.

The only fly reel that stands alone as far as I know is the Charlton Signature Series in titanium. Just the ticket for the biggest fish, and it's yours for $5,200. The only dolled-up touch is your signature engraved in gold on the reel, and that's not really out of place. I've seen the reel and I can't imagine how it could be improved. Mr. Charlton says they are impervious to everything and so it seems. I like the idea of something this exalted existing; it says something good, and rare, about taking an idea to the extreme, as good as man can possibly make it. I'd love to see one at work on a big tuna or be able to drag one out and pass it around when the camp talk turned to new "stuff." I'd be on the high ground for once.

Now that we've taken the rubber bands off the wallet, how about a new trout rod, something out of the ordinary? I give you the top of the heap: Thomas & Thomas' limited edition three-weight bamboo, with extra tip and leather case. They'll put your name on it for $3,800, which nicely avoids any mix-up at the lodge. Our good friends at Orvis have a nice selection of hand-crafted bamboo models at just under $1,600 each. I honestly doubt that these are profitable items, but are kept in the catalog because it's the right thing to do. Eventually the bamboo rod will vanish from all catalogs except those put together by auction houses, and it's unlikely that our grandchildren will ever see one close to running water. I know of several "name" makers' rods that have recently sold for over $10,000 each. I also remember not so long ago when they were sitting on the rack in any number of shops for a couple of hundred dollars.

Now one thing leads to one thing more: we need the perfect place to put our high-dollar toys to work. Kaufmann's Streamborn catalog lists a couple of private cottages on a private island in the Bahamas at $21,000 a week. Lest you demur too quickly, note that the price covers ten guests, food and drink, boats and guides, and just about anything else within reason. I'm ready to sign on as a break from my everyday routine of biscuits and cold water. After you do the arithmetic, and factor in a little something for splendor, it isn't too bad a deal.

Don't have ten friends? Like to fish alone? You can cast to forty-pound-and-better Atlantic salmon on the Alta River in Norway for about $15,000 a week. Don't forget airfare, a few extra flies, and a handsome tip for the gillie holding your fish of a lifetime.

I know you shotgunners are saying "What about me? Let me buy something!" Okay. Since we've just bought the Charlton reel, a Thomas & Thomas rod, taken our pals to the Bahamas, and then booked ourselves a restful week in Norway, we've dropped around $45,000. Sounds like a lot, but we've got some good stuff and times to show for it. What would the same shopping get you in a shotgun?

This is our lucky week. As a devotee of the 28-gauge and a believer that James Woodward made the best of the best English guns, I see that Criswell's latest catalog offers one of the rarest of the rare: A Woodward 28, straight stock, single trigger, and all the classic touches for a reasonable $49,000. If you're one of those worrywarts who'd be afraid to use things this valuable, think again. Barring disaster, the value won't be affected. I know that a lot of great stuff is treated like a commodity—something to be bought and sold. But I'd use all of this. I'd carry the Thomas & Thomas rod on the roughest pack trip, and take the Woodward in the dove and quail field until the bluing and checkering were indistinct. And if I had money left over after buying flies and shells, I'd get a sweatshirt made that said: "He who dies with the *best* toys wins."

31

THE ART OF
"HOW TO"

I happened across an old review of one of my books and the reviewer, although in general favorable to the stuff, remarked that what he liked most was that it wasn't larded with any "how to."

I was crushed. For years I've considered myself a master of the "how," sprinkling priceless tips around like salt in a heart-healthy diet—lightly enough to improve the flavor but not enough to be dangerous or spoil the taste.

I secretly prided myself as being the Emily Post of the outdoors. I have been a referee in matters of the heart, explaining to several young ladies that their husbands didn't really prefer the dog but that this is just an ancient masculine figure of speech. I have satisfactorily explained the arcane economic advantages of having a new shotgun and letting the old stove, rug, fridge, or whatever rest for another year. And best of all, I have passed on to others the most difficult "how to" of all—getting someone else to do it for you.

Personally, I have nothing against learning a new jigging technique for walleyes or nymphing for trout, but since I will be outfished in any event, I find it far more useful to praise the walleye expert—commenting on his carefully selected attire and the surgical precision of his handwork, for example—so that in the end, if you have done your work well, you will have a freezer full of walleye fillets.

This, if I may borrow from a different set of drummers, is the Zen of "how to." Why bother learning the Bimini Twist when experts are shoving each other out of the way to tie one for you to prove that they know how and you don't? Why bother to sharpen your knife when in your four-man tent three fellow Nimrods have brought eleven kinds of stones and exotic oils? By the second day they've sharpened all their stuff, including the kindling ax, and will grab hold of your knives like a preacher embracing a sinner.

A bit of high-level "how to" involves the tricks and techniques required to rationalize the purchase of a really expensive item such as an engraved and beautifully stocked gun. My essential approach to this (now espoused by Wall Street) is A Penny Saved Is Not Necessarily A Penny Earned. I recite parts of my own case history featuring the fact that I have almost never regretted buying something I couldn't afford. When you think about it, the real American Way, the thing that gives us a reason to dig in a little harder, shove our shoulders against a bigger wheel, is Debt. Debt sees no difference between the gun store and the orthodontist, although the latest rumor has it that Debt favors a matched pair of Woodwards to capped teeth; I can't swear to it. I have met Debt often, of course, but we've exchanged no more than small talk. I do have the feeling that he was very pleased with me.

When it comes to the more ordinary "how tos," I am something of a failure. Stubbornness and a lack of skill combine to keep me at a certain level, although

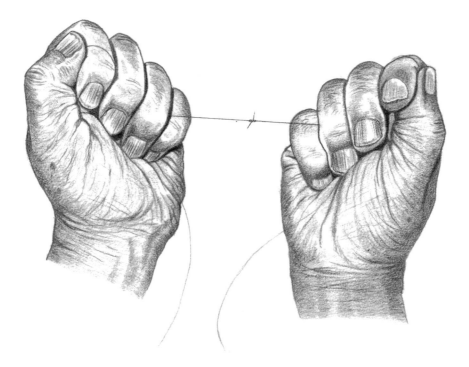

every now and then I do learn to tie a new knot. Too often the tips are just too, well, complicated. For example, I will lug a bag of mallard or widgeon decoys, and I will walk along with someone carrying an artificial hen turkey. But though I admit to having done some silly things in my deer hunting life, lugging a plastic doe ain't one of them.

The ordinary "how to" tips are supposed to be easy, but in reality they aren't. I'll give you three that I guarantee will work, but you won't take the advice in spite of that. Want to be a really better hunter? Learn to be quiet and to sit still. Want to be a better shot? Practice. Want to be a better fly caster? Practice. To be sure, some tips make a lot of sense, like the one about putting your wallet, etc., in a sealable plastic bag when you're out in the rain. But far too many tell you things like how to find North when you've lost your compass by poking a stick in the ground, tying a piece of string to it (you always have string, right?), doing something with the shadow of the string and your watch hour hand, and there you are. South is the opposite direction and the others are left and right. I have been lost and had no idea where I wanted to go even if I did know where North was.

A far more useful tip is that you should always tell someone where you're going when you go out alone. Unless, of course, you're going to a prime woodcock cover and the flight is down. You're not required to pass on *everything* you know.

32

THEY'RE NOT PLAYING OUR SONG

I was doing my laundry the other day when I remembered an old radio jingle that went "Rinso white, Rinso white...Happy little washday song."

This sordid imitation of the sweet call of the bobwhite quail depressed me as I sat waiting for the rinse cycle to end. I tried to recall any popular music dedicated to quail or ducks or pheasants, but I struck out. I did come up with lyrics having to do with swallows, wild geese, robins, bluebirds, even the wise old owl...but nothing on woodcock or grouse.

What about dogs? Even with my shabby memory, I came up with some hound dogs, some dogs of specific name, and just plain dogs, but there was no song of the setter or pointer, no foot-stomping beat that extolled the Labrador retriever or the honest beagle.

I find it hard to imagine that no troubadour ever put down his 12-gauge, picked up his guitar, and sang a ballad about Belle honoring Luke and Mr. Jones taking three birds on the covey rise. Think of the millions of hours idled away in duck blinds, surely some of them by men of musical bent. Yet no lyrical tribute to the shape of a decoy or the whistling of pintail wings exists, no popular story of Tar and his half-mile retrieve. There is no literature or verse that invokes the memory and deeds of our great shots. Fred Kimble alone ought to have stirred the poetic breast of dozens of creative people.

There are songs about the largemouth bass and even a light symphony that praises the trout. But in all honesty, avid fisherperson that I am, I just can't compare the slurp of a rainbow to the cackle of a cock pheasant. We have any number of poems about brooks and rivers, but who can deny the dark dignity and intrigue of a good swamp? The toe-tappers about corn and grain and apple trees are many, but who sings of the humble vines that shelter and feed partridge and quail? Where are the bards of the "Corn Crib Covey" or "The Woodcock Cover My Father Showed to Me"?

I don't know of a single good tune about rifles; there's plenty of meat there if anyone wanted to look. No verses make us yearn for Grandpa's L. C. Smith, or the Purdey at the end of the rainbow, or the long-lost Parker. "The Trapshooter's Lament" seems to be a natural. And what about the lonesome mother's plea for her wandering skeetshooter to please come home?

When you consider that the modern bamboo fly rod was created by a violin maker and that men have deceived their ladies and denied their children to acquire such equipment, why are there no laments naming Hiram Leonard or Pinky Gillum as home wreckers? Where are the true stories put to song about little girls standing by the banks of the Battenkill or the Madison—like "Father, Dear Father, Come Home With Me Now"? Or, "That Lovely Old Six-Weight of Mine"?

When you consider the pure romance of our outdoor adventures, and those odd but cherished moments of uncontrolled laughter or sad regret, you have to admit that much of this stuff ought to be preserved and handed down in rhythms that captivate the soul. Most of my companions own a banjo, harmonica, fiddle, or a guitar as well as shotguns, rods, rifles, and dogs. I'm not saying they are musicians, but they do play and they do keep their minds open in case something worthwhile thinking about should come along. Yet not one of them has taken the time to work up a good ballad to entertain folks like me who are of a serious bent and short of leisure time. How hard could it be to work up an idea like "The Pheasant in the Glen" or "Dixie's First Covey" or "Why Bill Won't Ever Get His Limit Anymore."

Since the average deer hunter can't sit still anyway and his imagination and daydreaming quotient is 2.8 times that of your average bird hunter, you'd think we'd have quartets of orange-hatted baritones belting out "I Got the Spike Buck Blues" or "She's Got a 7 mm Body and a .22 Mind." After all, it's these dreamers who gave us camo toilet paper and doe urine aftershave, so they must have more poetry left in their souls. Is there no Longfellow out there to entrance us with "Gone to the Great Treestand in the Sky"?

I don't know about you, but I could use a little relief from turkey-calling demonstrations at sportsmen's fundraising dinners. They only remind me how far away I am from ever making the things work. Or the Trout Unlimited gatherings where I have to look at slides from places I can't afford to go, showing trout I'm not smart enough to catch. Or field trial clubs where half the dogs demonstrating long retrieves or quadruple marks could have graduated from Yale.

Let's have music and song.

We could get up and dance "The Turkey Strut" or the "Pflueger Reel" with our sweetie-pie. Put our arms around each other and harmonize on "I'm a Double-Haulin' Momma and He's Just a Roll-Casting Man." Or how about one of everybody's old favorites: "I'm just a runner-up in the shoot-off of life, born to be second or third. If the guy I'm against is nervous and tense, it won't matter at least by a bird..."

Maybe if I hum a few bars...

33

New Eyes

Every now and then we need to rediscover some of the important things in life, to see the forest for the trees, to get unstuck. When bird covers become abstract and undefined, when trout no longer flash in the riffles, when a buck clearing a fence from a standing start fails to make you gasp with pleasure, it's time for *new eyes*.

It wasn't very long ago that *I* was the new eyes when I threw a fly at a tarpon the first time. The man who took me out had caught over a thousand of these great gamefish, yet my excitement when the tarpon struck my fly made him dance around the skiff like a small boy. He was seeing something again for the first time, remembering through me another very first cast. I had to cheer him up for quite a while when my tarpon broke off.

I've spent a lot of outdoor time giving others new eyes as they pass on their wisdom to me. When a good hunting guide realizes you want to be something more than just a man lugging a rifle, he will show you an inner woods where the bear steals honey and the winds bounce off a sun-warmed cliff, and he'll explain why a bull elk feeds here instead of there—and why the stand you choose won't work and the one he picks just might. I want to learn this not just for myself, but to have some store of things to pass along, to share through someone else's new eyes.

I would enjoy new eyes to hunt deer because I love the chase I learned from others years ago, but I don't feel the need to take another buck myself just now. I'd like to have someone care as much as I once did about tracking snow, a perfect stand, the magic of seeing something where there was nothing only a moment ago or the faint sound of steps that make the woods come alive. It's important to help someone learn that hunting is both an art and a craft, and that the shot is often the least of it.

New eyes on a good salmon river would remind me once again how much I care about these special waters which both fight and shelter the fish. It would be good to talk to someone "fresh" about the merits of a Lady Amherst vs. a Dusty Miller, to make me dust off my memories and dwell a bit on the magic of a fish that lives years of its life in the ocean and returns unerringly to the gravel bed where it was born.

I'd like to share a dove with the new eyes of a shotgunner, remembering all too well the odd mixture of frustration at being so inept at something and delight in every minute of it at exactly the same time. And I'd like to take someone new to woodcock to a classic cover and share, too, the strange blend of sorrow and joy when the dog brings one of the birds back to hand—the paradox of success in the hunting field.

I remember my first grouse, taken all alone by the purest blend of accident and luck, and how carefully and casually I laid it out on the counter of the country store where I had stopped, ostensibly to buy another half-dozen shells. The old hands wanted to know the how and where, and until I saw them smile at my excited story I didn't realize how much it pleased them to see in my new eyes what they could recall of their first bird; I was handing back something that time had nearly hidden away.

When I was a small boy running a famously inefficient trapline, my father would often come along with me to check the sets. I dreaded these outings almost as much as I welcomed them. He was forever stopping me and asking, "What's been digging at these leaves?" I'd gather my tiny knowledge of leaf-disturbing creatures and hope I was at least close.

"I think it's been a skunk digging for grubs." My father, pained at my ignorance, would point out the small pawprints and the vertical burrowing and patiently explain that it was a squirrel digging up something he's buried.

"Common sense is all it takes," he'd tell me, and I would fear that common sense was not one of my strong points and see my planned career as a frontier trapper dwindling before my careless eyes. It was only his way of being a boy again, hearing the same things from his father, remembering it all with unspoken pleasure. He needed new eyes to see his world—a sharing of love in the shy and quiet way of the country man.

And then there are the indoor pleasures, the favorite books that take us to places we haven't seen or bring us back to see it one more time. In the pages of these books things live forever—the tales of the high-country hunters, the grouse and woodcock stories in clipped New England prose, the memories of Mississippi duck camps, and the soft voices of the South that talk of Mr. Bob. The legends of the Catskills, "Tricks That Take Big Bass," and the sea hunters in search of the giant billfish and tuna.

New eyes are like puppies to old dogs. They give us a feeling that what we've done is worthwhile because they believe it. The importance that we once knew about the right way to build a fire, set a tent, start a bird dog, row a boat reconfirms itself when we do it for someone who sees it or learns it for the first time. When a person new to the outdoors discovers that being warm and dry and catching fish or taking birds isn't just pure chance, that woodcraft and skill and practice are all a part of the things we care so much about, it adds a new edge of pleasure to so many things we've grown to take for granted. Another dawn in a duck blind can still be one of the great experiences of our lives, especially when we show it to others.

Not long ago I talked a friend into buying his first skeet gun, and I'm sure I'll learn again, as I should, a lot of the things I've grown careless about. His new eyes will sharpen mine. And another friend talked me into getting some new stuff so he can introduce me to his favorite steelhead river; he's at least as excited about it as I am. So it should be, since the experiences we all treasure are renewable. Every puppy is almost our first dog, and every new gun or rod or place is the chance to have a fresh start. I know of little else in life that offers so much promise as that.

This business of showing a set of new eyes such fine points as where the trout lie and why and where the buck is most likely to step into the clearing is not something only old-timers can enjoy. At almost any time a person with something to share can open that door to someone else, and have the great pleasure of feeling the wonder of it all again, of knowing that he's done what comes close to magic, and most important, turned a pilgrim into a true believer.

34

THE

MYSTERY FISH

I've been lucky enough to have fished enough water and to have read enough books and been with enough experts to arrive at the conclusion that none of us knows a whole lot about Atlantic salmon fishing.

The basic casting techniques are simple enough in most instances to be learned in a short time. The obfuscation of terminology is a lot less confusing and off-putting than you find in your average trout "how-to" treatise, and since the fish isn't feeding, the choice of flies is more often than not dictated by whim or prejudice or luck. Certain rivers, according to tradition, fish best with "favorite" flies. The magnificent Lady Amherst is still a favorite on the Grand Caspedia, while a few miles away, the guides on the Matapedia insist on a Rusty Rat first, and then might give way to a Green Highlander or Cosseboom. Nearby, on the Restigouche, I'd lean toward a Dusty Miller or Roger's Fancy. And on and on. One famous fisherman on Scotland's Spey River ties on a March Brown and fishes until he loses it or has an idea that one of a different size might be a touch better. On the Mirimachee you'd better show up with some Conrads or Green Butts, or be quickly labeled either weird or a know-nothing.

Yet, the real charm of fishing for salmon is that very little is chiseled in stone. Here is the ideal sport for someone like myself who likes big water and the chance for a big fish, and who doesn't get too bored with the thought of having to make X-to-the-tenth power of casts before something happens. I don't even have to know the names of more than four or five fly patterns, and I can rest easy as long as I can tell the difference between a bright fly and a dark one—and I'm not at all convinced that is critical. I do like big flies in heavy or cold water and small ones when the rivers are low and warm, but I have seen a lot of fish taken by anglers who espouse a completely reverse strategy.

When it comes to the dry fly, I have to admit that the most successful surface worker on the rivers I've fished most has been the Bomber. How I wish it weren't so! The Bomber looks like someone tried to imitate the butt of an inferior cigar; and the more nondescript and gross, the greater its appeal. I don't know how many times I've drifted exquisite Skater or Wulff or Irresistible patterns over a bored salmon, only to have it come to life with a vengeance when I reluctantly went to the Bomber. Needless to say, theories abound with learned observations about fishing "in the film" to the "generic memory" of a certain bug, to salmon "taking" a fly in anger or in defense of territory, or whatever, but your guess is just about as valid as anyone's. I doubt if the salmon all have the same reason for jumping on a Bomber, but you can be reasonably sure that it is the closest thing to *the* sure-fire dry fly—preferably in a plain brown tie.

None of this is meant to imply that any of us goes to a river with just a handful of flies. Tradition insists that a great deal of time be spent both on the water and in camp arguing about patterns and sizes. Fly boxes must be opened and passed around, and flies must be held up to the light and admired, especially the handsome, fully dressed English patterns, in spite of ample evidence that they don't fish as well as the homelier and simpler local hair-wing creations. Indeed, homeliness often seems to be a plus when it comes to salmon flies.

I believe that if there were no endless mysteries, the salmon would be just another interesting fish. There would be no books lovingly written and filled with charts and diagrams and color plates of lovely flies. There would be no river maps to tuck in your vest so you can pinpoint where the salmon held in 1904 or thereabouts. There would be no magic in the waters called Grimsa, Alta, Tweed, St. Jean, or Tay, and no reverence for the intricate art by reel makers like vom Hofe or Bogdan or Zwarg. We would have no reason to dream of fish in pools called Friday's Farm, Toad Brook, or Lady Slipper. Old fishermen would eventually just "not be here" instead of having been "called to *The Home Pool.*" There would be no stories that end with "the guide swore it was over forty," or "just then the net broke," or "he pointed to the Major's famous hen fish over the fireplace, and said, 'I'll swear it was the twin to that one...'"

Endless speculation and frustrating flailing on rivers blurred red by sunsets or silvered by morning mist are part of salmon fishing. It's a game of chance in which grizzled men look up to make a wish on a star, or cast with their fingers crossed, or carry a lucky stone from a river that once yielded a silver leaper. "Secret" flies, hidden moves with line and rod learned from a famous gillie in Scotland or an Indian guide in Quebec, are very important. Salmon fishing is an act of faith, a pilgrimage, a worshipping of the unknown by the unknowing.

If I could close my eyes and wish for a dream to come true, I would open them on a pool in a big river I will not name. Here, under some giant spruce, hidden behind boulders and ledges, is a tiny trickle of ice-cold spring water seeping into the river. You might fish this piece of water for years and never know about the little spring where the salmon lie with their noses up against the freshet like a hay-time farm boy holding his head underneath a hand pump. If a salmon could smile, this is the time and place it would happen.

At dinner in this wishful dream I would hold up my "magic fly" and tell the captive faces at the table how years of experience and technique all fell into place, and how the guide had whispered reverently, "*Dix kilos*" (twenty-two pounds) as he released the fish. I am that rare and envied sportsman, knowledgeable about the ways of salmon and willing to share what I have learned with this doting group of would-be salmon catchers.

But dreams don't last forever. This one ends when everyone suddenly begins to laugh...

35

WISH LIST

I've already bought myself a Christmas present—just in case. I got in the habit because I never found any expensive fly reels or four-weight rods or 28-gauge shotguns under the tree in spite of being good all year and leaving magazine articles, catalogs, and other such suggestive materials lying around.

A lot of women aren't into stuff like that even though they tend to do the bulk of their shopping before Christmas Eve. I think they do this to avoid being in the stores with a bunch of men like me holding up stuff and trying to remember if the lady is a size 5 or a Small and if they're approximately the same thing. One of the reasons men buy women things like vacuum cleaners and electric skillets is that they don't have to worry about sizes and colors.

I feel obligated to remind the ladies that men don't like new clothes. If you buy a man a new sweater, for example, the first thing he does is tug at it to pull it all out of shape so it looks like the one the puppy sleeps on. Men also don't like colors that range far from tan or brown. All men want to look alike; they have the same outfits for the D.U. dinner, the T.U. outings, the gun club, or washing the pickup. Why women don't see that is a mystery to me. Neckties don't count since men just grab one and have no idea what is on it other than birds, dogs, and food stains. Some ties have trout flies or fish on them, but they are not as all-purpose as pheasant or mallard ties.

A man doesn't even like to wear a new flannel shirt out in public. He'll try to sneak it into the wash or wear it around the place in secret until it's properly shabby. The best time to wear a new shirt is when you are training the Labrador to do water retrieves in the rain. Same with new pants. Men do not even know their sizes. All men are size Large at least; if it's too big, that's fine; if it's too small, their feelings are hurt and it stays in the dresser forever. This is especially true of belts; all men are either size 36 or 38 if you ask them, but anything smaller than a size 40 will probably end up as a leash or a flushing whip.

Men will not take anything back to the store and exchange it. They don't know how this works and they feel guilty about even considering it. Exchanging things means talking to salespersons, which is something else men won't do—even if they're buying stuff for themselves. If a man buys something for himself that doesn't look right or fit properly, he will just throw it away, like a bad poker hand. Men don't like to shop with women because women always ask men to try things on to make sure they fit. But men don't know if things fit and don't care; the only size criteria is "big enough."

A woman will ask me, "What do you think Larry wants for Christmas?" I might reply, "He wants a new four-weight fly rod." She says he already has a fly rod and I say that doesn't make any difference because by virtue of its *newness*, a *new* rod is better than the old one. Actually, Larry probably has *three* four-weight rods for the reason I just outlined, but this defies feminine logic. I could point out to his wife that she probably has three identical (as far as her husband is concerned) blue dresses, and would not look askance at yet another, but I do not do this because I have learned not to do so. The hard way.

My own (unfulfilled) Christmas list doesn't change much from year to year; a case of trap loads, a dozen Royal Wulffs, a nifty fly box with my name on it so it might get returned when I drop it on the streambank. A wading staff, also with my name on it for the same reason. A case of skeet loads, 28-gauge. A tie with a pheasant or fly pattern. A flashlight. A wind-up alarm clock. A four-weight rod and a good reel to go with it, complete with line. Shooting glasses. Binoculars...But along about now, the lady is looking over my shoulder with glazed eyes. A month from now, she'll be asking, "Where's that nice pink sweater I bought you for Christmas?"

If the average man is asked what he really wants for Christmas, he will answer, "Nothing much." Most women are delighted to take this literally. I don't blame them, either. The man in question appears to be outfitted rather adequately. Only an in-depth investigation will reveal that the poor soul is trying to find a way to bring a set of Briley tubes into the breakfast chitchat or lead into a discussion about the need for an adjustable stock for the trap gun and head off any further discussion about linoleum or gas ranges. But he is afraid that his wife thinks Briley tubes are part of his anatomy and discussions of adjustable stocks might conjure up bleak images of wobbly finances.

At any rate, I will be delighted to parade around the place on Christmas morning in my new bathrobe, tugging at the hem of my pink sweater, knowing that my package from Briley has already arrived in a discreet brown wrapper and that the lady won't mind that I also gave myself a new four-weight. Maybe she'll even smile and hand me a reel to go with it.

36

DEEP
THOUGHTS

In our fishing literature, water gurgles, grumbles, shoves, pulls, frightens, soothes, beckons, and calls. But rarely is the dimension of sheer depth discussed.

Deep water is eerie to me, mysterious and full of myth, like strange voices in the night. Not long ago I had to smile at myself when I asked a mate on a fishing boat how deep it was (as I always do) and he said it was over a thousand feet and I started edging away from the side of the boat as I might have stepped back from a skyscraper window.

In my mind I will always equate deep water with big fish, even when I know I'm wrong. A Quebec river I used to fish for salmon has an enormously deep hole cut into a dark rock face that's so dark and haunting it seems almost supernatural. I cannot pass it by, no matter what the guide says about salmon lies notwithstanding. No, I never had a salmon take there, nor probably has anyone else, but it still quickens my pulse to see the current suck a fly down deep out of sight. If you were to imagine the Throne Room of the Salmon King, it might look very much like this deep lair.

No matter where you grew up, I'll bet that there was some sort of "bottomless" hole, perhaps an abandoned quarry, reputed to hold a child-eating bass, a yard-long pickerel, or some such monster of the deep. My local mystery lake, forbidden by all parents for fishing or swimming, graduated from surface green to deep black, and small boys knew that once below the surface, all hope was gone. Of course I fished it, pitching a Pflueger Chum to the far side and watching it tinkle down out of sight before I began the slow and tantalizing retrieve. It was like a flashlight in a strange dark room where you were really more in hope of *not* seeing something.

But every so often something touches us from the dark world of the deep. Hemingway once wrote about fighting an eighty-pound white marlin that was suddenly grabbed by "something" and pulled down into the great depths. The helpless Hemingway hung on and as suddenly as it had gone, the marlin came back up. It was squeezed absolutely flat for a couple of feet in its mid-section and by the shape of the mouth marks, the guess was that it had been seized by another marlin, a marlin so big there was nothing to measure it against.

Many years ago, I had the same sort of thing happen to me when I lost a huge lake trout—or was it a pike?—in northern Manitoba. It's an odd feeling and one that shrinks you down to size a bit. It's that "something" fish we all somehow knew was there, the unseen shadow under every bait we troll.

As a boy, most often fishing alone, I did a lot of trolling on a local lake. I used two or three rods fanned out across the stern, and I worked the oars at a funereal pace to make sure that the June Bug spinner with its tag of pork rind, the live frog, and the River Runt or Hawaiian Wiggler were scouring the very depths of Little Lake, where the big ones were. No one else ever fished there, but I never wondered why. I don't recall ever catching anything worthwhile, but I do know that I always had that certain strange feeling: this might just be the day...

A large part of the magnetism of deep water is its very darkness. We can put anything we want in a place where we can't see, and what better place than the depths, hidden from the light, unseen from above. A deep-cut bank must be like being in bed with a blanket over your head. A great, deep hole is a secret room, where the light no longer reaches behind a closed door. Safety in the dark depths.

Fishing the deep dark places is, for the most part, best done at night, adding a degree of difficulty that I have never really come to grips with. While I can cast a plug well in the dark, fly fishing is impossible; I only know where my fly is when it's in a tree or my jacket. But I fly fish at night anyway; if you walk out before the last of the night, when the major actors are about to take the stage, you are missing an important part of the show.

My deep-water fly-fishing efforts have been, to be honest, mostly nonproductive. Big fish do lie in the depths, but they are wise fish and my weighted Matuka or Woolly Bugger doesn't even amuse them anymore. But I do have one fish story!

For my "last cast" before leaving a long, dark, and deep salmon pool, I tied on something big and black and let it sink until the line went slack. Then I slowly ticked the fly along the bottom, the way you'd fish a rubber worm. When the salmon took, I was lucky the rod wasn't ripped from my hand, and before I could believe it, my whole fly line was off the reel and at the very end of the pool. By then it was totally dark and I couldn't see to wade below the fish. Knowing better, I pulled, not gently enough, to start him back up the pool so I could gain line.

Not to happen. A great shake of the head and I pulled in a straightened out #4 fly. I never saw the fish, but it sits on my memory wall just the same, reminding me of places deep and dark, places that are not without hope.

37

BIG-GAME
FISHING

I have found that most of us who throw a fly for the first time to a fish in the 100-pound class do so with some misgivings. It's a step into the unknown where anything can happen, and often does.

The transition from *normal* fly fishing, including "big" salmon or steelhead, to the world of fish five feet long, and longer, begins with tackle. Going from an eight- or nine-weight rod to an eleven, twelve, or thirteen-weight is a giant step indeed. The big rods are judicious compromises between casting instruments and long hoists to lever huge disputatious fish from where they want to be to where you want them to be, and this often has both comical and disastrous results. Big-game fly reels are also impressive; my tarpon reel weighs about a pound and a quarter.

With this tackle, the so-called simple act of casting takes on a new dimension. The fly is bigger, heavier, and a lot more wind resistant. The line is rope-like, and the days when the wind isn't brisk and off your wrong shoulder are so few as to be negligible. You are absolutely, positively going to have to learn to double haul, really double haul—among other tricks. You don't "hunt bear with a switch."

On the other hand, you usually don't have to do a lot of casting, since most of the time you'll only be throwing to fish you see. I like to stand on the boat and practice cast, knowing that I need to. I'll also do a fair amount of blind casting if I think there are enough fish passing by so it might be productive; most of the time it isn't, but I have taken a few doing this.

Like almost everyone else, I started "big fishing" for tarpon in the Florida Keys. In my mind the Everglades Bay area is one of the most beautiful and interesting places on earth. A group of highly competent professional guides work this productive tarpon water and will do their very best to put you into fish and teach you how to deal with them. In the Keys guides do their thing in a very patient and skillful way—and if anyone has ever tested their forbearance, it's me. When you learn how to throw a fly to a string of six-foot tarpon, almost anything can happen. And whatever does happen will be unforgettable.

Fishing the Florida "flats" combines the elements of finding the fish, stalking them, and presenting the fly. The parallel between big-game hunting and big-game fishing is obvious, including all the things that can go wrong. Except that here, at the end of one of the few times that everything goes the way you had hoped, you turn the fish loose and wish it well.

Big tarpon also swim along the coasts of Mexico, the Atlantic side of Central America, and down to Ven-

Countrysport Press

*Please send me a free copy of the current Countrysport catalogue
of fine sporting books and art.*

Name _____ Telephone _____

Address _____

City/State _____ Zip _____

Also send a copy of the catalogue to:

Name _____ Telephone _____

Address _____

City/State _____ Zip _____

or call 800-367-4177 to request a catalog

COUNTRYSPORT PRESS
CRAIG INDUSTRIAL PARK
BUILDING 116
SELMA, AL 36701

ezuela, and fly fishermen are increasingly seeking them there and in Gulf of Mexico waters, off of Florida, Louisiana, and Texas.

Having gotten thoroughly involved with big fish fever, I recently took another bite out of the apple. At the insistence of several more experienced saltwater fly fishers, I found myself making up good, sensible, and practical reasons why it was totally necessary to go to Costa Rica's Pacific Coast for sailfish and marlin. The general attitude was "if you think tarpon are exciting... just wait."

Billfish roam in deeper water than tarpon, about 100 fathoms (600 feet), where they can locate schools of baitfish and squid. But they can be easily teased up to the surface with a trolled bait, or "teaser," skidding along the top. When a billfish comes to the teaser, the mate "plays" with it until it is about forty feet away from the stern of the boat. Then he lofts the teaser out of the water, the captain throws the boat in neutral, and the angler casts the fly. Hopefully, the billfish hits it.

I freely admit that all this is not fly fishing in its purest sense, but a billfish in the air is one of the most exciting spectacles in sport.

The equipment is identical to tarpon fishing. The rod is a twelve- or thirteen-weight and the saltwater fly reel holds 300 to 400 yards of thirty-pound-test backing. The leader, according to the rules of the International Game Fishing Association, must have a section at least fifteen inches long that tests no more than sixteen pounds, but there's no reason not to go to heavier stuff if records aren't your bag. The billfish fly is a creation that runs about six to ten inches long. I leave it to your imagination about how interesting it is to cast, but it's easier than it sounds.

At a place called Bahia Pez Vela (Spanish for Sailfish Bay), I got lucky and caught a couple of Pacific sails, each a bit over 100 pounds—but not until I'd lost several fish. It seems my "learning curve" is not as short as most. Then, at 8:55 A.M. on July 22, as I was throwing the fly to a teased sailfish, a blue marlin shouldered the smaller sail aside and got the hook.

I have never felt so insignificant and helpless in all my years of fishing. For almost an hour the great fish—the captain figured it was over 200 pounds—did just about as it pleased. I like to think that he was playing me as much as I thought I was playing him, and that the explosive, spinning leaps, the silver sides flashing like a strobe, the deep thrusting runs toward the bottom that spooled off 300 yards of line, were a show of brute force that would intimidate and mock me—as they did. Finally, the 100-pound-test shock leader parted, probably cut in the sharp corner of the marlin's jaw.

As I reeled in the slack line, feeling more privileged than disappointed, I heard the mate say something and saw him point. Out against the morning sun, a huge blue marlin leaped and fell, and leaped again and again. I like to think it was "my" fish, joyous in victory.

"Forever and forever farewell...this parting was well made..."

38

MISSING

SOUNDS

I've never really feared being hard of hearing because I grew up that way. The trouble is that it gets worse. I've learned to adapt and consider the problem more of an annoyance than an affliction. I can't say that the people who spend a lot of time repeating what they've said to me would agree, but there it is.

My earliest memories of the farmhouse dining table are of great-uncles with Old Testament names—Obediah, Zerah, and the like—sitting there with their hands cupped behind their ears, looking questioningly at each other or nodding politely during conversations full of missing words. They were pleasant gentlemen and I felt sorry for them. I'm glad I was understanding because now it's my turn.

A small boy who had a little trouble hearing wasn't much to worry about in my day. When I got scolded for staring out the classroom window instead of answering "Harrisburg" when asked the capitol of Pennsylvania, it was because I was a daydreamer. It never occurred to anyone, me included, that some voices and pitches were hard for me to handle.

Of course, I started shooting long before anyone thought of any kind of hearing protection. I can't remember when I didn't have a gun of some kind, and when I had shells I shot them up. Each round probably took a small toll. Even in my beginning days of trap and skeet, the most sensitive shooters didn't do much more than stuff a little cotton in their ears, which was at best an affectation. I didn't even do that, and I ended up with a ringing in the ears that finally stayed. I did seek help until one fairly famous and frank specialist told me: "Don't waste any more money on hearing examinations. As you get older it will get worse and there's nothing you can do about it." My only real regret was that if I'd sought him out earlier, I could have saved enough money to buy a higher grade of trap gun.

As you know, the hunter is captive to his hearing. The woods are an orchestra where a false note disturbs everything. As a sometime big game hunter, I have lost several chances at deer and elk simply because I was so dependent on eyesight that I never heard the hordes parading around behind me or a bit off to one side. A lot of professional hunters in Africa are no better off with hearing than I am, and so I became quite diffident about taking on very dangerous game. I'd been in too many places where I couldn't *see* a Cape buffalo or a lion just a few yards away, let alone *hear* one. And I know all too well what happens to the hearing I still have in the few moments after firing a round or two in my .375.

Bird hunting is different. The dogs give me a point of reference and I've learned that since I have to look for something, I shoot a little slower. I solved that by going to a bit more choke in my bird guns, and I do as well as the next average wingshot. Actually I may do

a little better because being "surprised" by birds seems to keep me from the evils of tracking, aiming, and several other faults I've mastered.

Fishing is supposed to be a quiet pastime, so I get along just fine on the water. I can safely ignore the catalog of useless advice and banter (what is more idiotic than your buddy shouting, "Don't lose him!") and respond only to important questions like "How about a cold drink?"; "I think you're caught up in the top of that willow"; or, when I'm in a small metal boat, "Did you hear a little thunder?"

I once took my canoe over a small power dam because I didn't hear the falls below. But since it seemed to amuse a couple of bystanders, I pretended that I did it on purpose.

On the positive side, I don't have to listen to trapshooters tell me why they missed two targets from station five—or even worse, hear why they think I muffed two targets from station five. I don't miss being kept awake by dogs barking at the moon, either. And I can sleep through average or moderate snoring in camp. I can pretend I didn't hear the telephone and I always let someone else ask for directions when we're lost because I never get them straight anyway. Guides let me walk the road in heavy grouse and woodcock covers because they don't think I'll hear flushes; I get the open cover deer stands for the same reason.

The negative side has its lighter moments, or so some people think. Wading a stream in Alaska, I got the warning confused about a big log floating down behind me. And there was the time when the guide whispered something about a bear just around the corner...But as I've said, if these things strike some people as funny, I can go along with it.

There are many things worse than losing a bit of hearing. If the deepening shadows that fall on the ear mute some of the important songs, we can always rely on memory, or imagination. When I see a bull elk throw back his head and trumpet his "Long Live the King" notes, I know just what they sound like even though they are too distant for my ear. I listen with my mind and, nicely enough, this lets me hear what I want, when I want, even though the sounds are not always there— like the *bob-white* in my meadow years after the quail have gone.

Where distance permits, it is the custom of Scottish pipers to begin playing from a distance too remote to be heard. They march, pushing the wild notes before them, until the far off listener picks up *something* in the air and the pipers, led by their own music, march into view. They leave the same way until they are lost from sight, and the music, almost too light to still be real, fills the emptiness.

I hear now sounds in the woods that may or may not be there. Hopeful that they may signal the footsteps of a buck or the strutting of a great bearded tom, I wait, not knowing whether I am listening to new sounds arriving, or sounds of the past—tunes remembered but not heard.

39

CANVASBACKS

The canvasback, sadly one of the most depleted of our North American ducks, was originally created to inspire the handsomest of all working decoys and, when it was legal to take them in numbers, gluttony.

The diminution of the canvasback is due to several factors. Two of the most interesting are a whim of nature that brings forth more males than females, leading to considerable bickering during courtship, and the fact that the artistry of the decoy has always proved as irresistible to the duck as it has to duck hunters. No matter how pathetic a wingshot was (and I personally know how pathetic that can be), if he had enough patience, northeast winds, and shells, he could count on a duck dinner.

And canvasbacks were *the* duck dinner! Even the most indifferent Eastern Shore bride could toss a brace in a roasting pan and serve up a meal half an hour later that grown men would fight over. Put into the hands of a sensitive chef, the canvasback could achieve an aura bordering on the sacred, as it did in fine old establishments like the Eager House in Baltimore. Thick damask napkins a yard square were tucked in the hard, starched collars of serious trenchermen. Close at hand

would be a bottle of Maryland rye whisky and a sampling of fine beer. There would be a robust Bordeaux or Burgundy rich with the threat of gout, tureens of terrapin soup, dozens of musky Chincoteague oysters, platters of cornbread and biscuits, a saddle of hare, perhaps a woodcock or two. And then, with appetites just slightly edged for the fullest appreciation, came the canvasbacks.

There would be wild rice, a thin sauce redolent of brandy, wine, and orange bitters, and oven-roasted potatoes, brussel sprouts, and sugar-glazed carrots, all followed by a trolley of cheeses, after which came another trolley of delicate and less than delicate sweets. To ensure digestion, there would be a glass or two of port or Madeira and a passing of hand-rolled, chocolate-colored pure Havana cigars, each as thick as a sashweight.

The men who provided the canvasbacks for such as the Eager House knew port only as a nautical position, and might place Maderia as the capitol of Spain. Their concern with the canvasbacks was as exotic as that of the gourmands, but their utensils were different. They wielded 10-gauge side-by-sides with outside hammers and English addresses on the barrels and, near the end of it all, pump-action Winchesters and semi-automatic Remingtons and Brownings with magazine extensions that ran right up to the end of the muzzle.

They gunned from pungeys, deadeyes, sneak skiffs, and sink boxes that were as cold and deadly as coffins. They gunned from them by lantern light, moonlight, and in ice-shrouded fog so thick that the only direction they knew for sure was straight down. They gunned for money, they said. But as long as the canvasbacks swept down to the celery-covered Susquehanna flats of the Chesapeake Bay, the gunners spoke of them with a tone in their voice and a light in their eye that had little to do with cash. They called themselves *baymen* with a soft pride that is bought with the copper taste of fear and marked by the scars that come to all who battle with the sea. It was a way of life a whole lot more than a way of making a living.

Of course they all thought it could never end. There would always be the low flocks scudding across the chop like whirling clouds, the live callers, the 300 block rigs, and the empty barrels waiting to be filled and trucked to the fanciest hotels in New York, Chicago, and Boston.

Then, suddenly, the wild celery and the eelgrass were gone and so was the canvasback, and the decoys and the silver tureens, and a way of life.

I was in the Chesapeake country a few years ago and stopped to ask directions. There was a pile of decoys in the back of an open shed.

"Those yours?" I asked.

"Used to be," the man said. "They're Cathy's now."

"What does she do with them?" I asked.

"Kindling," was all he said.

Then he went over to the pile, picked out a decoy, and gave it to me. He didn't say *here take one* or anything, and I didn't say *thank you* or anything. It was a moment more like a funeral than one of gift giving, and when I waved goodbye he didn't wave back.

Some little museums still have displays of the time of the canvasback. Punt guns, corn oil lanterns, salt scoured skiffs, and the like are set off with sepia pictures of formal-looking men dressed in hip boots and oilskins and holding shotguns. These displays are rarely crowded and for a minute or two you can stand there and hear the slap of the chop, the low pitch of the wind and the high notes of the wings, and the strange *brr-brr* sound of the ducks circling. There is the sound of the hammers being cocked and then the last seconds of silence as the muzzles swing up from the hide and sort through the flock looking for possible pairs and triples.

I look at the hard faces of the nameless men in those faded photographs, and I can see myself. I know it's wrong now, but how I would have loved it then!

40

LOSS OF
HABITAT

One of the little local gun clubs that I care a lot about will soon disappear, a victim of the same fate that a lot of our ducks face: loss of habitat.

The club was a lovely place to spend a Sunday. The members and their guests enjoyed the warm talk of guns and shooting and the stories of hunting trips past and future. We gossiped, told jokes, and reveled in each other's company. It was everything a little gun club ought to be, part of the heartbeat of American shooting.

Small gun clubs have always come and gone. The men grow old and the boys move away. But there was usually someplace else to go on to, another club down the road where the fragments of one group joined up with another, holding things together for a while at least.

Most of us got started at little clubs. It didn't cost much to shoot, there wasn't much competitive pressure, and a twenty-five straight was the exception, not the rule. These were casual places where you had a chance to fool with something different like a borrowed Parker or Ithaca or Fox, loaned with pride and pleasure. In time we learned what we thought we needed to know about stocks and triggers and balance, and if all went well, we traded or sold or bought this or that until we had something that seemed to work—at least for a while.

As far as I can remember, I shot at my first clay target at a firehouse picnic. In late autumn, just before hunting season, that was the way small towns raised money: a deadmark turkey shoot at fifty cents or a dollar a chance, which bought you five or ten targets from a hand-cranked trap hidden behind an old door resting on a couple of hay bales. A score of eight or nine was usually good for a prize, which was often a chicken or a flashlight. The guns were what you'd classify as "farm equipment"—cheap Lefevers and Bakers and other $50 side-by-sides. All the owners bragged about the full patterns their guns threw and tales were told about this fox or that deer "at a solid eighty paces, maybe more!"

I dearly loved those shoots. The local ladies made the lunch and sold pies and cakes and cookies, and all of us heavy eaters made the most of it. If you traveled the fall fire company circuit and managed to break better than three-quarters of the targets thrown, you ended up as a shotgunner to be reckoned with. I won a plastic trophy once—probably with a score of nine since I always got too nervous and usually missed my last target—and enjoyed a brief but satisfying glory as a "ringer."

The small towns grew and the fire departments found more sophisticated ways to raise money. By this time I was a "regular trapshooter" with a real trap gun of my own and a membership in a nearby little club. It wasn't much more sophisticated than the traveling trap that made the rounds of the firehouse outings, but at least we had a real clubhouse, two fields, and a rather plain but much prized jacket patch. It was the sort of club I like because you belonged instead of just being a member. We painted the houses and mowed the lawn and cooked the lunch, and often there was a treat from one of the members—some smoked fish or a bushel of oysters or a tray of cookies baked by a wife who understood the importance of being at the club on shooting days. In time I moved away. I heard that some ground was sold and the new neighbors complained about the noise and theoretical danger, and then the club was gone. Loss of habitat one more time.

I continued to shoot a little trap and the odd round of skeet at a variety of places, none close enough to consider joining as a regular member or even to visit frequently. The ideal club ought to be close to home, kind of small, and competitive only on a very minor scale, a place where shooting and such were a part of the talk but not all of it—a place where friendship and camaraderie are predominant. My little club fit the bill perfectly and it's hard to say goodbye.

I feel sorry for myself and the rest of the members, of course. We are losing a heritage of a special sportsmanship and the coming crop of youngsters in the area won't have a place to go to learn firsthand, as we did, about wildlife and conservation. That loss is immeasurable and infinite and probably irreplaceable.

I suspect the old trophies and fading photographs will end up in an attic somewhere, and in time someone will hold up a picture of a group of strangers standing proudly with shotguns and then, without regret or curiosity, throw it out—loss of habitat cuts a pretty broad swath.

I know we'll have quite a party on the last day. We'll unquestionably make plans to meet here and there, but that too will fade. The blade of the bulldozer will be crushing a lot more than shingles and siding. But to all us castaways, the little club will be remembered with a very special, almost secret fondness, like the memory of that closest boyhood friend who long ago moved away.

41

ANOTHER
DOG?

"When are you going to get another dog?"

"Not for a while," I answer; "It wouldn't be practical right now."

The memories of my last dog are still sharp, and as with any good friend, you tend to recall the peculiarities as fondly as whatever degree of "quality" you used to boast about. As time passes and the place grows emptier, it's almost impossible to admit that the torn edges of the rug were once a cause for anger. The old chair where she liked to perch—in order to keep an eye on me and be first at the door when I wanted to go outside—didn't look right so I've filled it up with books. It's just a piece of furniture now, no longer a "place."

I can't say how often I've come *this close* to hiring myself out to another dog. But every time I get right to the edge, I back off. If I'm thinking Labrador, then I wonder if I ought to have an English pointer, or another Brittany, or maybe a little Jack Russell just for company. And then I realize that what I'm really looking for is something I can't have, because she was crushed by a careless driver at the end of the lane where she was waiting for me.

All of my excuses are honest, or so I keep telling myself. I travel too much to have another dog. I don't have the time or the ambition to do the basic training. Most of my gunning friends already have dogs. I don't really do all that much bird hunting anymore, and with the duck situation what it is, who needs a retriever for just two or three birds? It just isn't practical...

I must admit that there *have* been moments when I stopped and looked back hopefully, at an empty path for a friend trotting along in my footsteps. But a new dog just really wouldn't be practical. It would probably chew on the chair legs, mess the rug, bark at night, dig holes in the lawn, and jump up on me when I came home. It would want to sleep by my bed, ride in the car when I ran errands, follow me around all the time, and put its head on my lap when I was trying to read. It would want to go along in the boat if I was fishing, retrieve unbroken targets from the hand trap, sit under my chair at the table in case I accidentally dropped something. It might even cry and whine when I left it alone, forcing me to invent reasons to take it along *all* the time, not just when we go gunning.

It's not only the inconvenience; it's the money. First it's the little puppy collars, the tiny training bumpers, and the squeaky toys and leather bones. I've heard that sometimes a pup will even chew a shoe, and that's expensive unless you let the dog have both shoes and just forget it. When the dog is a bit older you need another dog bed, so you have one in the kitchen and one in the bedroom, and those things aren't cheap. Then you have to go for larger collars, maybe a leash with the dog's name on it, bigger training bumpers, a blank pistol, a kennel for the station wagon, and maybe a station wagon if you don't already have one.

I can't see how you can get by without some new briar pants, chaps, hip boots, parka, and foul-weather gear if you're going to take the dog outside. You might even need a new shotgun, or perhaps two, and what's the point of having shotguns if there's no place to fool with them, so add on gun club costs and maybe a little something for the local shooting preserve. If you're going to do it, you really can't cut the basic corners. And as a practical person, I've kept all this to the minimum.

But it's too much trouble for me to even consider. What with weekends spent training, there wouldn't be time to paint the back of the garage and I'd be fooling with the dog when I had any time off instead of visiting relatives or doing other good works. I actually know people who consider their dog a member of the family and sign its name to birthday cards, display pictures of it all over the house, and refuse to have anybody over who isn't as crazy about *Spike* as they are. Would you believe doormats with dogs on them? Fireplace irons that look like dogs? Dog Christmas cards? There are things you wouldn't believe people do just over a dog.

I've got a lot of better things to do with my time and money than fool with another dog. But if anything unforeseen happens, one of those unfortunate situations that you can't escape, when there's absolutely no way out and I get saddled with a dog against my better judgment, I might possibly name it Maggie. That would really be quite practical. You see, I already have a leash and a dog dish with the name Maggie on them. It wouldn't have been good sense to have thrown them away.

42

DAYS
GONE BY

Maybe it's just me, but when I think of ducks I think of a *lot* of them; the great flights like smoke with no beginning and no end that I once saw in Manitoba, or the endless rafts that blanketed Barnegat Bay, or the deafening sound of mallards tumbling down through the flooded Arkansas timber. I remember the stories about the old clubs and the market gunners, and the pictures of derby-hatted sports holding huge double guns and leaning against the side of their open touring car, behind triple rows of birds.

There won't be many stories from our generation. The duck clubs are mostly gone and I probably couldn't find a decent derby if I felt like sporting one, just for the feel of it.

The old, hand-laid-up gunning boats are museum pieces, and decent decoys are called "folk art" and priced accordingly. Your average Labrador retriever is accustomed to being ferried around in a fancy four-wheel drive, and the closest most of them will ever get to a bird feather is sneaking up on the master's pillow. As much as I like sporting clays, I wouldn't dream of getting up at 3 A.M. and standing around in a sleet storm to shoot a round.

No, I haven't quit the blind or tossed my insulated waders on the trash heap. But I feel like the fat man who has notes pinned all over the fridge about going easy on the sweets—a lot of the fun has gone out of a favorite pastime. I don't mind taking less; what bothers me is that it's not my choice anymore.

The worst thing is that no one seems to have any answers. The "habitat" crowd says there is a shortage of ponds, marshes, and ditches. The "numbers" people say there's plenty of room at the inn, but we just don't have any customers. We can't do very much about either situation and we are left scratching our heads and digging down to buy duck stamps and hunting licenses in the hope that somehow, something will happen and we'll wake up and find that the problems have disappeared like a bad dream. I remember that when I could see ducks that were almost numberless, I worried about the lack of Canada geese and whitetail deer, both of which are now virtually pests in my part of the country. Good game management fixed that, and I still have hope that our wildlife people will come through yet again. I have more than hope—I have faith.

In the meantime, I'm adjusting, or trying to. It's not that I ever liked to take all the ducks I was entitled to; a limit was more than I wanted for my occasional roast mallard dinner. What I liked most about being out there was the good feeling, the absolute richness of seeing plenty of broadbills, pintails, widgeon, teal, and mallards and their various relatives. A big outdoor party is better than a little one; more laughter and gossip, more news—more excitement.

I would often just sit in my blind long after I had the few birds I wanted just to listen and watch. I really don't know why. I certainly wasn't learning anything and I doubt if sitting in a sub-zero wind on a rough plank talking to a retriever is a sign of superior intelligence, but I spent a lot of time doing just that. It made me feel good not to shoot even when I could have. My perceived skill with a shotgun always rises immensely when the gun is empty—there is absolutely no flinching or poking or stopping as I swing past a long quartering angle on a sliding drake and hear the pins fall on a pair of dead shells. "Beat that, Mr. Kimble!" I say, as a pair of fifty-yard greenheads make an imaginary tumble to the soundless report of my imaginary best London double.

I have a strong belief that the duck hunter is probably the best example of sustained childhood in the sporting world. When my grandson jumps up and down in a mud puddle, I still want to do it too. And I know just how I can with no one raising an eyebrow. Where else can a grown man put on hip boots and take his dog and go play in the water and have most of the people who know what he's doing not laugh at him? What other excuse is half as good for having a little boat and a real motor in a huge bathtub? How about making a lot of silly noise with a duck call at the same time! And maybe even having a special 4WD truck so you can drive where you want, and probably shouldn't, which is why it has a winch on the front bumper.

In my heart, I want to believe that what we are now going through is one of those things we can't scientifically explain and so label a "cycle." I think that more than any other wild game, ducks are symbols of freedom. We like to follow them with the mind of the dreamer, wishing that we too could take wing and leave our barren places for more lush and exciting ones. Somehow the duck exemplifies a bit of very enviable irresponsibility, doing just enough to get by and flying off to more glamorous pursuits whenever the mood strikes, as if daring us to do the very same.

The grown man stands by the window watching the clouds carry the promise of what the old-timers called *weather*. The prudent voice calls to him to fetch some dry wood for the evening fire, and listening to the wind outside, he hears the far-off calling and he knows that the high flocks are leaning back, coasting with the wind and having a joy ride. Another voice, one from his childhood, speaks to him now, calling for hip boots and a gunning coat. The dog which ignored the trip to the woodpile has heard it too, and stands waiting by the door.

43

SEARCHING

Not long ago I got a letter from a man who was looking for a lost dog. He described the emptiness of his days and nights, the hopelessness, the guilt, the hurt in his heart, and the inability to understand why so much of his life had been captured forever by what most other people would call "just a dog."

We who have been there, listening in the night and stopping strangers on the road in the day, know something of this. We know the ache inside, the cruel silence that follows the calling of a name; the sucking quiet that flows over us as we stand there hearing only the break in our voice as we question the dark with *Duke...Duke...*and then take a step or so farther into the void to throw the call deeper...the little bit of distance that might make the difference.

Not knowing is worse than death; not knowing is pain with no end, no possibility of forgetfulness; not knowing is timeless; not knowing takes forever to wear itself out. When we bury a dog we know what to bury with it and what we can keep alive in our secret places. The hopeful savage in us all sends our friend off to a better place with a favorite blanket, a rag or slipper, an empty shotgun shell or two. We have a place to visit when we need to summon up a better time, whisper a word or two, or take the small comfort that can come from giving a warm pat to a cold stone, or dropping a few feathers to mingle with fallen leaves.

The lost dog is a different torture. Never again, so it seems, can we drive or walk without looking at everything and listening to what might ride on the wind. Every nighttime bark is a summons to pain; every dog we ever see is subject to scrutiny. Who do you talk to? Who do you tell? Who really cares? Who can see "just another dog" for what it really was to you? How can you really describe it when asked what it looked like?

"Just a plain black Lab with a little spot of white on the chest. Kind of a small dog, really—be kind of hard to spot in a crowd," you say, remembering the way he looked at you with his head cocked a little to one side as if ready to smile and the funny throaty sounds he made when you talked to him on a long ride with his head in your lap; the way he waited for you at the head of the lane and raced the truck down the drive-way; the way he'd carry your hunting hat when you "accidentally" dropped it, or shamelessly begged for the extra cookie you always brought for him. You remember that he knew how to wipe his feet on the door mat and tug at your pants leg when he was tired and wanted you to come upstairs to bed. "Just your ordinary plain black Lab," you say and walk away.

A lost dog becomes something different. What faults it had seem to diminish and its strengths and charm become more endearing, like a child that's no longer home. We see the lost dog as helpless without us, and searching for us as passionately as we search for it.

That's what our heart says. What really happens is often something else. I think that now and then certain dogs revert, for some unknown reason, to virtual wildness, and become a creature of thousands of years past. Some just plain outrun their brains and panic, much as a human will do. No doubt some just don't care as much as we thought they did and they find themselves satisfied to wander where their spirit moves; staying here or there for a bit and then moving, their relationship with man growing more and more tenuous with time. And some are just plain lost and will look at every man and listen to every passing car waiting for the familiar name, the special sound that calls them home.

I don't ever remember not seeing, in my small hometown, some sign tacked to a utility pole, some note pinned to the store bulletin board, a handmade flier in my mailbox, with the pleading and urgent words *Lost Dog*. The prodigal creature is always gentle, a member of the family; the words carry a tone of puzzled sadness...a feeling of how could this happen...please hurry.

Nor do I ever remember a sign or note or flier telling of a happy ending, saying that Freckles is back home and that all of those who kept an eye out for her are thanked for caring.

I saw a handsome dog just the other day, walking along the roadside with a determined air. He didn't seem "lost"; he was wearing a collar, but he certainly wasn't the companion of anyone I could see. Was he one of the legion of lost dogs with an anxious master stuffing mailboxes, or was he a free spirit, an adventurer, a creature who felt he was treated badly or misunderstood? Was he hoping someone would find him or was he hoping to find someone else? If a familiar voice called his name which way would he turn?

Out of curiosity and compassion I read the *Lost Dog* notes in the local store; nothing matched the wayfarer I'd seen. Like people, some dogs are lost and others are looking for new lives—or trying to.

44

PERFECTION

Someone once wrote that a perfect day of fishing would mean stalking a particular fish, discovering what it was taking, making one perfect cast, and having the little devil. Needless to say, that has never happened to me, but I'm not sure that would be my idea of a perfect day anyway.

Perfect days vary according to the mood and the place and other unexplainable factors. Sometimes you don't know you've had a perfect day until it's over.

I had a perfect day in late March a year ago. I was in Islamorada in the Florida Keys during one of the cold and windy spells that seem to follow me, especially when I have tarpon on my mind. The guides were as dour as the weather, but I finally badgered my old friend Captain Jimmie Albright into taking me out in the afternoon. I'm sure he was tired of listening to me and figured if we were out on the water, I'd cast more and chatter less.

And for once, *it* happened. We struggled through a light chop to the edge of a flat. No sooner had we arrived than the wind stopped and the water turned dead calm. As far as we could see, large tarpon were rolling and basking. Jimmie poled close to a huge fish we'd seen "laying up." I made one cast and was hooked up to a fish we estimated to be better than 130 pounds. I'm not sure the fish realized it was hooked—at least it didn't take the fact too seriously—but it jumped about six or eight times, rolling its great shoulders like an arrogant wrestler, and after almost an hour simply shook out the hook.

Neither one of us said anything for a few minutes. I had a cold beer and just sat there smiling, seeing the great fish held in the air forever and glowing from the magic of being so incredibly alive, glowing from this transfusion of wonder.

"That's as good as it ever gets," Jimmie said. "You can hook up to 100 and somehow one or two will stick in your mind forever. That's why we do it—for the one that we take home in our mind."

By now the wind had come back up and the bay was empty, as if there had never been anything there. We rode back in a small sea, and every so often the crest of a broken wave would wash my face and I'd turn around and Jimmie would smile at me and I'd smile back.

A workable definition of a perfect day is one that you never forget, a day saved by *something* that seems to get lodged in the mind so it can be recalled when urgently needed. It could be a day like the one I spent with Fred Webb on New Brunswick's Tobique.

We sat in a canoe in a bucketing rain casting for salmon only because we couldn't think of any acceptable reason not to. It was pleasantly uncomfortable, if you know what I mean.

I've forgotten whether or not we took any fish, but I do remember that late in the afternoon a baby moose waded out in the river to join us. The little calf came with no hesitation whatever, as if it had been waiting for us. It marched out in that odd step moose have, stuck its nose over the gunwale, and looked at us as if waiting for words of wisdom.

Fred, always the practical woodsman, asked of the whereabouts of his mother. I asked if there were any salmon about. The moose looked carefully at each of us and then, obviously disappointed at our lack of wit and charm, turned and left. I had again been given a gift, a surprise that I had wanted but hadn't known it. I'm not sure exactly what I saw in those few minutes of moose magic, but I was certainly charmed, and perhaps even given an insight that I'm just not smart enough to fully understand.

If a perfect day can be simply memorable, then my day of days was when I lost nine consecutive Atlantic salmon. (If you're not a salmon fisherman, let me say that any time you catch or even hook one salmon a day on average in any salmon water is very, very good indeed.) I will gloss over all the reasons I lost so many fish because I want to retain some self-esteem and because of my unwillingness to blame external events over which I have no control. I will tell you how determined I was not to lose the last fish, a rather small one of about five pounds or so. Alone, with no net, I let this fish seek refuge beneath a slight cut bank, convinced I could grab the salmon by the tail and so snatch a small victory from the great gaping jaws of defeat. I put the rod down on the bank—I was fishing from the shore without boots—and reached under the bank. I was doing fairly well working my hand close enough to take a death grip when for reasons known only to the Almighty, the section of the bank I was leaning over suddenly let go and I slid with both grace and elegance face first into the stream. Even I know when to quit and keep my mouth shut; I'm only going public with this to make a splash, so to speak.

A perfect day is often measured in minutes and sometimes only seconds. A good example is that rare cast to a rising fish ordinarily beyond our modest reach, when the timing of the double haul and the lift of a sweet breeze sends the fly out to a rarified distance, with the loops as tight as a clothespin, the fly tugging at the backing knot and then drifting down on the water as softly as a wish. Such a cast might even solicit a perfect passing remark from an acquaintance possessed of the highest casting skills and long a subject of envy— "I see you're getting the full measure of the rod. Very nicely done." Flattered beyond reason I foolishly try to outdo myself and spend the next few minutes secretly changing the snarled tippet under the guise of bending on another fly. Perfect days must occasionally be shared, though they may be nonetheless memorable—like the day I took a personal best, a thirty-two-pound salmon, only to arrive at the dock and see a crowd around Tom Hennessey and his forty-pounder. I have just recently forgiven him.

I never plan on perfect days, since my expectations and my skills are forever separated by an unbridgeable chasm. Not long ago, I was fly fishing a trout stream with some friends. My casting technique was pretty good, if I do say so myself, until I stepped on an unseen rock. A full minute later I surfaced, to a round of applause from my "friends" on the bank. They gave me two nines and an eight. I still think I deserved tens across the board, but that's what you get when you fish with people who have so little grace and style that they don't recognize perfection when they see it!

45

DAYDREAMS

From the blind, set up with its front feet in the water, I look out over a small pond churned into a turbid brown by paddling Canada geese. It's not a real pond, just a shallow, scooped-out cup that will be plowed in for spring planting. But I like it here, as strange as that may seem for a man who likes to think of himself as a hunter.

Beyond the pond, no more than half a mile, there is an old farmhouse, its crumbling brick walls losing their hold on each other—the way old things let go— and gently sliding back into the clay where they started. Close to the farmhouse is the skeleton of a clapboard room held together by its chimney spine. They tell me it was once the township school. I tell them I once went to a school much like this one and they look at me a little oddly, but I really did. And I can still remember the sounds of recess and the games we played with no more than a ball and stick, cheered on by the barking of the farm dogs that walked us to school, brought back the balls we batted out of the tiny schoolyard, shared our lunch, and then walked us home again.

Little flocks of geese drift like rising smoke over the tilted chimney. I know they won't come to a call, but since I'm alone, I blow it just the same. The sound of it seems to shove the geese even farther away, the way good singers, those with correct pitch, used to edge away from me when I sang in Sunday school.

It's unsettling to see the same geese I just frightened circle low over a shopping mall and drop into a graze field where they feed under harrows and plows left for the winter, quarreling over spilled silage just a few yards from a busy farmyard.

Wildness is a state of mind. "My" geese are wild when they're far enough away in the sky to be abstract and my mind is up there with them, but not down here where I listen to long-ago voices from a barely remembered childhood. Everything reaches a compromise; neither the geese nor I listen to the sounds of traffic, just to each other, as if we're both pretending things are not as they are but how they ought to be. The geese are here because this is where they have always been at this time of the year, and I am here because *they* are.

One of the things I like about hunting is *thinking* about what I'm hunting, mulling questions I can't answer. I like not knowing why a flock of geese, feeding and gossiping in a tattered cornfield, will suddenly, for no reason I can fathom, stop and raise their heads as one, and then fly. Not randomly as you and I might run in opposite ways when frightened but thoughtfully, purposefully, and precisely. And then, just as mysteriously, they will circle once or twice and land right back in the same corn rows—or form a long flared V, like a giant feathered arrow, and disappear into nothingness.

I have tried walking, bold and noisy, up on a bunch of feeding geese in an open field, and several times I have gotten well into gun range. I have also hidden in a blind so well concealed you'd be hard put to see it until you nearly fell over it, with a spread of 100 perfectly placed decoys and an expert caller turning himself blue in the face, and watched flock after flock of geese circle once or twice and then go silently away.

They say you have to be as smart as a goose to take any. I'm not but I have, and I don't really know much more about the whole operation than I ever did. And that's one of the reasons I'm out there so often, as innocent of knowledge as a babe and just as content. *Maybe something right will happen* is about all the heavy thinking I can bring to bear on a day in a goose blind— no different from all the hunters before me and no different, I hope and trust, from all the hunters that will come along in future time.

Geese are not gifted with reason and logic; they merely respond with nothing more complicated than simple instinct and its variations of fear and trust. While some of us are more skilled callers than others, so are others more gifted wingshots or more able to sit still and be patient.

I am more than fair when it comes to goose hunting. I violate, knowingly, all the tenets I ought to observe. I fidget, I look up when I shouldn't, I call even though I know better—no matter how hard I practice, it sounds "like a cat in a trap" according to one of my guides. I tell him I'm a very selective gunner, just going after the really dumb ones.

I tend to daydream. Just before dark, a pair of Canadas slip into the pond before I see them. They roll and splash, having a recess of their own on the wet edge of the old school yard. I decide to wait for them to leave of their own accord; they are like a soft hand on my shoulder and I can't bring myself to frighten them.

Other geese are sliding overhead and their calling seems to come from behind the stars, thin and distant and chill. My pond geese pay no attention, but I am inspired. Asking silent forgiveness of my friend Jim Olt, I begin to honk, doing my very best. The geese stop splashing, look around, and then, unhurriedly but surely, swim to the far side of the pond, walk up into the field, and disappear into the night.

I pack my stuff, leave the blind, and stand for a minute at the edge of the pond. I am tempted to call out into the darkness something I remember from Thoreau: *"The woods would be very silent if no birds sang except those that sing best."* But I don't. Why waste a good line when there's no one listening.

46

GONE
FISHING

I've got two new fly rods and they're scratching at the door to go out. I'm feeling my "fiddlefoot" mood; the urge to travel is running pretty high.

I used to believe—because I wanted to—that the farther you travel, the bigger the fish and the more of them. But since I've gotten the *big* and the *plenty* parts out of my system, I'm down to what *really* makes me want to go over the mountain or around the far bend to see where the trail might lead.

Just the names of places I want to visit offer promises of discovery. The Rogue, the Battenkill, the Spey, the Restigouche, Okechobee, Great Bear. Waters named after kings, hopes, Indian visions, lost settlers, or explorers who might have been heading off the edge of the earth for all they knew. Places that affect your mind, places where you go fishing to catch one thing and often end up with something else.

Stand in a river in the West and before long you can actually sense the presence of Sioux or Cheyenne warriors. And you can hear the ghosts of a regimental band playing, with great gusto and pride, "The Yellow Rose of Texas" and then the back-straightening musical fire of "Garry Owen."

From somewhere you can't quite make out comes the shuffle of hooves, the creak of army saddles, and the bark of a sergeant at a young soldier who day-dreams, remembering a farmside brook far away, and wondering about just where General Yellowhair might be taking him this time. Perhaps he'd get a chance to use the hook and line he had tucked away in his saddlebag.

I also like to visit places where it all began in Yankee Country, where the people with that clipped, waste-not-want-not accent once put freedom on the scale, weighed what it would cost, and paid dearly for it. The people haven't changed much in the small villages along the cold mountain streams with Dutch and English names. You can easily imagine what they might have thought about fishing just for the pleasure of it. A lot of them probably still think that way. I always stop and look at the little cannon mounted on granite in the town square and read the names from 1777 and see the same names from the early 1860s, 1917, World War II, Korea, and Vietnam. Still watering the tree of liberty.

From the bridge I watch a handful of small trout sipping on something and it's easy to imagine a rather thin and sallow man picking through a fly box. I can hear the local boys talking about Mr. Theodore Gordon and his "flies" with mixed wonder and disbelief. You have to smile when you think about it, because after all the science and Latin, it boils down to the fact that there is still a nice piece of pure magic about trout fishing with flies. Clambering down the bank to have a closer look, I wonder what Mr. Gordon would have floated over these fish.

You can do a lot of pleasant things in Scotland on a Sunday, but you can't fish for salmon. I met my gillie for breakfast and then we took a long walk afterward. I teased him about the Sunday law, saying that the church still holds the high ground.

"No, no, it's not that at all," he replied. "We're just resting the water."

We spent a delightful day together, not far from the town where my mother's family left for the New World almost 200 years ago. The next few days I spent trying to learn the Spey cast with my borrowed fourteen-foot rod—alarming the sheep too foolhardy to avoid the riverbanks and thrashing the salmon out of pool after pool. I remember having a wonderful time, but I'm not sure if I caught more than one or two fish. I like to think I did, but I wouldn't bet on it.

Back home they'll ask, "Been fishing again?" And I tell them that I have. "What did you catch?" I usually answer something like, "A handful of this and that," and most people are satisfied. A fellow fisherman might want to know more and the talk can turn to flies and tides and boats and such. But I keep the part about hearing a band play over the sound of the wind on a western river or seeing a redheaded woman in the little market in a Scottish village who looked enough like my mother to almost frighten me...all to myself.